MOZART'S
Thematic Catalogue

A FACSIMILE

Verzeichnüß

aller meiner Werke

vom Monath febraio 1784 bis Monath

Wolfgang Amadè Mozart

MOZART'S
Thematic Catalogue

A FACSIMILE

British Library
Stefan Zweig MS 63

*Introduction
and transcription by*
ALBI ROSENTHAL
&
ALAN TYSON

THE BRITISH LIBRARY

Frontispiece
Front cover of Mozart's Thematic Catalogue.
British Library, Stefan Zweig MS 63.

© 1990 The British Library Board

First published 1990 by
The British Library
Great Russell Street
London WC1B 3DG

British Library Cataloguing in Publication Data
Mozart, Wolfgang Amadeus, *1756–1791*
    Mozart's thematic catalogue : a Facsimile : British
    Library Stefan Zweig MS 63.
    1. Austrian music. Mozart, Wolfgang Amadeus, 1756–1791
    I. Title II. British Library
    780.92

    ISBN 0 7123 0202 6

Designed by John Mitchell
Typeset in Linotronic 300 Bembo
by Bexhill Phototypesetters, Bexhill-on-Sea
Origination by York House Graphics, Hanwell
Printed in England by The Roundwood Press (Southam) Ltd.

CONTENTS

THE HISTORY OF MOZART'S *THEMATIC CATALOGUE*
by Albi Rosenthal
page 3

DESCRIPTION OF THE MANUSCRIPT
by Alan Tyson
page 11

TRANSCRIPTION OF MOZART'S ENTRIES
by Alan Tyson
page 27

THE FACSIMILE
page 59

Portrait of Mozart.
Drawn at Dresden by Doris Stock,
March or April 1789.
Reproduced to original size.

THE HISTORY OF MOZART'S *THEMATIC CATALOGUE*

W.A. MOZART's own *Catalogue* of his works, begun in 1784 and kept up to date by him until three weeks before his death in 1791, is here reproduced in facsimile in its entirety for the first time.[1] The unique significance and fascination of the volume, both as a musical and biographical source, have been fully recognised since it was first mentioned in writing by Constanze, Mozart's widow, in her correspondence with Breitkopf & Härtel, the Leipzig music publishers, in 1798. Franz Niemetschek, whose Life of Mozart (*Leben des k.k.Kapellmeisters Wolfgang Gottlieb Mozart*) was published in the same year, had been given access to it by Constanze while writing his biography.

On 8 November 1799, Johann Anton André (1774–1842), who had just succeeded his father Johann André as head of the music publishing firm of 'Johann André' in Offenbach, signed a contract with Constanze, in Vienna, whereby he purchased from her for his firm all extant manuscripts of Mozart in her possession, pledging to send her four free copies of each work as they came from the press. Johann André and his firm had been well known to Mozart, who took the opportunity of visiting his friend in nearby Offenbach during his stay in Frankfurt in 1790. 'Clad in a grey travel coat with short collar, Mozart stopped in front of the André house. No sooner had he alighted from the coach than he was attracted by dance

---

1   A generally very good facsimile was published in an edition of 200 copies by Herbert Reichner in Vienna in 1938, together with a booklet of explanatory notes by O.E. Deutsch. It was reissued from New York by the same publisher in 1956, with an English version of O.E. Deutsch's text. That facsimile did not, however, as does the present one, reproduce the blank but fully stave-ruled pages following Mozart's final entry on 15 November 1791, which are in themselves a poignant comment on the tragedy of Mozart's early death.

music: the male and female workers of the firm had been given permission to hold a dance. Mozart mixed with them quickly, chose the prettiest girl and danced with her for a long time to his heart's content . . .'.[2] J. Anton André, the then 16 year old son, attended a rehearsal for 'Don Giovanni' in Mannheim at the end of October of that year, when Mozart complained about Kapellmeister Fränzl's slow tempi and asked for livelier ones. He described Mozart as 'a small, nervous man of rather pallid complexion, but with reddish cheeks and with a prominent, large nose'.

After Mozart's death on 5 December 1791 at the age of 35, his fame spread internationally to a degree far beyond his renown during his lifetime. It is not surprising that the knowledge of the existence of a large number of manuscripts of unknown and unpublished compositions, aroused widespread curiosity and expectation throughout the musical world. Even before J. Anton André came upon the scene, Constanze had been in touch with other publishers concerning the publication of the manuscripts in her possession, Johann Traeg of Vienna and Breitkopf & Härtel of Leipzig amongst them (the latter, particularly, with considerable success). It was André, however, who secured the bulk of Mozart's original manuscripts in 1799.

The catalogue of compositions, the present 'Verzeichnüss aller meiner Werke . . .' (hereafter referred to as the *Catalogue*), written by Mozart himself in the last six and three-quarter years of his life was, of course, of enormous significance and value to any publisher. Constanze had guarded it jealously and had refused to make it available to Breitkopf & Härtel, though she had mentioned its existence in several letters to them in 1798 and 1799. On 8 January 1800, two months after signing the contract of sale, she wrote to André: 'aside from the number of parcels, you are getting one more packet containing my husband's thematic catalogue, a few other lists, etc.' On 15 February she informed Breitkopf & Härtel of this: 'Herr André had to promise me to publish a complete thematic catalogue . . . which you will receive in due course. The publication of it would in my opinion crown the biography'. On 21 February she wrote again to André: 'I look forward with infinite expectation to the complete thematic catalogue, as agreed . . .'.

J. Anton André, himself an accomplished musician and music scholar, had indeed envisaged the publication of a complete chronologically

---

2   A.H. André, *Zur Geschichte der Familie André*, Garmisch, 1963, p.113.

arranged thematic catalogue of *all* manuscripts in the 'Nachlass', that is to say of every work from Mozart's earliest compositions to the last. He soon realised, however, that this was far too big a task to undertake, as the cataloguing in chronological order of the 250 manuscripts written before Mozart began his *Catalogue* in 1784, a great number of which were undated, would be a labour of very many years. Mozart himself would have found it an onerous task to arrange so large a number of his earlier manuscripts chronologically in retrospect, even if he had wanted to do so, which is highly unlikely: his sister Maria Anna ('Nannerl') wrote in a letter of 4 August 1799: 'my brother appreciated his older works less and less, the more he advanced in composition'.

The publication of a faithful transcript of the *Catalogue* of 1784 to 1791 became, therefore, the most urgent and indeed only feasible project: it would reveal to the public the number and nature of works for eventual publication by the firm, and would, in addition, provide biographers with a chronological record of Mozart's immense productivity during the period covered by the catalogue, his 'golden years'.

Constanze wrote of it to André on 29 March 1800: 'the catalogue was, from its inception, kept so accurately by Mozart, that he carefully entered even the small things he wrote on his journeys, e.g. the small Gigue he composed in Leipzig in 1789'. In June 1799 she had written: 'It may be that Mozart composed more Lieder after 1784 than are noted down in his thematic catalogue: hardly, however, more than one or two, as he apparently took his catalogue with him on his journeys for this purpose. Thus the Gigue, as well as things composed in Berlin, are entered under the headings "Leipzig" and "Potsdam" in their correct chronological sequence'. The appendix to Nikolaus von Nissen's *Biographie W.A. Mozarts*, 1828, edited by Constanze, contains a note after the abbreviated (without incipits) reprint of the *Catalogue*: 'In those years (1784–1791) Mozart composed much else that he did not enter in this Verzeichnis and that cannot be performed, as he presented quite a few such things to friends without having retained a copy for himself'. Opinions have since varied as to the completeness of the *Catalogue* (see the discussion of its contents on pp. 11–25 below).

While it has been claimed that Mozart's *Catalogue* is unique among a composer's own records, thematic catalogues had been in existence well before he adopted this system. The term 'thematic catalogue' was first used in print by the music publisher J.J. Hummel in 1768. The most famous series are the printed catalogues issued periodically by Breitkopf & Härtel in Leipzig between 1762 and 1787, advertising upwards of 14,000 works, with their musical incipits (opening themes), available in manuscript or printed form through their firm. Mozart is likely to have been familiar with this widely distributed catalogue.

Leopold Mozart made a list of Wolfgang's youthful compositions in 1768: 'Catalogue of all the things that this 12 year old youngster composed since his seventh year . . .' ('Verzeichniss alles desjenigen was dieser 12 jährige Knab seit seinem 7ten Jahre componiert . . .').[3] This list has no incipits. Another list of Wolfgang's works, with incipits, was offered by Leopold to Padre Martini on 22 December 1777: 'I have yet another idea, namely to send you the incipits of his compositions, beginning with his sonatas for the harpsichord composed for Madame Victoire . . .' [K.6 and 7] ('. . . ho ancora un'altra idea, cioé di mandargli il principio delle sue composizioni, cominciando dalle sue sonate per il cembalo composte per Madame Victoire . . .'). This list is lost, if indeed it was ever written, or received by Padre Martini in Bologna. The original manuscripts of nine early symphonies of Mozart (Nos. 22–30) dating from 1773 to 1774, sold at auction in 1987 and now deposited in the Pierpont Morgan Library, New York, were gathered together and bound into one volume, in grey wrappers, by Leopold Mozart in the 1770s; he wrote a thematic list of contents on the front cover, which, except for the deliberate absence of dates and somewhat shorter musical incipits, is essentially similar to Mozart's *Catalogue* (fig. 1). It may well be, therefore, that the impetus for keeping a catalogue with incipits originated with Leopold. Mozart stayed with him on a visit to Salzburg until 27 October 1783, only three and a half months before the date of the first entry in the *Catalogue*. The unprecedented increase in Mozart's activities, both as composer and performer, from the beginning of 1784 onwards, would have been reason enough for him to keep the kind of diary of his compositions which the *Catalogue* represents. Mozart also began keeping exact accounts of his income (takings at his concerts, fees for lessons, sales of works, and the like) and expenditure, in March 1784, almost exactly at the moment in his life when he started chronicling his compositions systematically. His financial accounting continued for only one year, was then taken over by Constanze, and soon abandoned altogether. By contrast, the record of his works was continued faithfully, if at times fitfully, for the rest of his life.

---

3   Paris, BN Conservatoire MS 2630.

6

Fig. 1   *Front cover of the volume of manuscripts of Mozart's Symphonies Nos. 22–30, with the thematic list of contents made by Leopold Mozart in the 1770s. (Reproduced by kind permission of Sotheby's, London and the Pierpont Morgan Library, New York.)*

The first printed edition of the *Catalogue* was published by André in 1805 (fig.2). It is not only a remarkably accurate printed version of Mozart's manuscript, adhering to the arrangement, text, number of pages and staves in the original layout (only a French translation of the text was added), but it is also a significant document in the history of printing, being the first book produced by the new process of lithography. Aloys Senefelder and Franz Gleissner, its originators, had been called by André from Munich to Offenbach in 1799. The lithographic method was refined

Fig. 2   *Title page of André's 1805 printed edition. British Library, Hirsch IV. 1062.*

8

there, and became widely used for music and graphics in consequence. Franz Gleissner was also employed by André in checking Mozart's manuscripts, which he marked, usually in red ink, and it is possible that some of the markings in the *Catalogue* were made during the process of checking its entries against the manuscripts.

In the brief Preface to this 1805 edition, André announces that apart from the works entered by Mozart in this *Catalogue*, there were about 250 earlier manuscripts in his possession, making 450 in all: he would in due course publish a separate chronological thematic catalogue of these as well. He mentions how fascinating he found the perusal of Mozart's original manuscripts, revealing, as they did, the original disposition and subsequent elaboration of his ideas. Most of the scores, he writes, particularly from the mid-1770s onward, are written very neatly, with small notes, fully shaped, and without signs of hesitation. André is reported to have been so fascinated by the beauty and revelations of these manuscripts that he was dilatory in publishing them, devoting a great deal of time to their analysis and study: this was the reason why Breitkopf & Härtel, to whom Constanze had sent manuscript copies of many of Mozart's autograph manuscripts, particularly of music for the piano, before 1799, were quicker in publishing them than André. The fruits of André's studies are revealed in his Prefaces to some of the published editions over the ensuing decades, which are scholarly and perspicacious, and anticipate modern musicological methods of research.

In a more elaborate Preface to the second printed edition (1828) of the *Catalogue*, now called *Thematischer Catalog*, André expresses regret that he had still not been able to publish a chronological catalogue of the pre-1784 manuscripts, announced in the 1805 edition and promised to Constanze as early as 15 February 1800. This catalogue was finally completed in 1833, but was never published. A copy of it is in the British Library.[4] Together with the *Catalogue* and the manuscripts themselves, it became one of the principal sources for Ludwig Ritter von Köchel's *Chronologisch-thematisches Verzeichnis sämtlicher Tonwerke Wolfgang Amadé Mozarts*, 1862.[5]

A final thematic catalogue, prepared for André by his young assistant Heinrich Henkel was printed in 1841, a year before J. Anton André's death.

---

4   British Library Add.MS 32142.
5   Leopold Mozart's list of his son's early works, together with the *Catalogue* and André's lists were first published in English in abbreviated form in Edward Holmes, *The Life of Mozart*, London, Chapman and Hall, 1845, p.355–364.

It was not arranged chronologically, but by categories (Church Music, Operas, Concert Arias, Songs, Symphonies, and so on). By then, the catalogue was needed as part of André's attempts to interest the libraries of Berlin, Vienna, London, and others in the possible acquisition of the entire archive. These were unsuccessful, and in 1854 the collection, including the *Catalogue*, was distributed among the heirs, six sons and one son-in-law. The major part of the manuscripts was eventually acquired by the Royal Library, Berlin, in 1873. The remainder was sold in two auctions held in Berlin by the firm of Leo Liepmannssohn: the first of these, on 12 October 1929, contained the *Catalogue* (lot 17), the second and final auction took place on 9 December, 1932. In both auctions many lots remained unsold; the Wall Street crash and the subsequent financial crisis had caused a generally depressed state of the international, particularly the German, economy, which had a highly restraining effect on private and public collecting. The *Catalogue*, estimated at 36,000 Marks, did not reach this figure at the auction and remained unsold.

It was eventually sold, in 1935, by private treaty to Stefan Zweig who regarded it as the most precious of all his musical treasures, no doubt rightly so. Having remained with his heirs in London, and been deposited by them on loan at the British Museum in 1956, the *Catalogue* was finally presented, together with their other musical and literary manuscripts, to the British Library in 1986.

Even 200 years after it was written, problems of interpretation regarding entries in the *Catalogue* remain, as is demonstrated in the following pages. This facsimile edition, on the other hand, gives us an immediate and illuminating insight into Mozart's miraculous productivity, and, through the features of his handwriting, into facets of his enigmatic personality. It will enable the musical public worldwide to examine and enjoy this unique document in musical history and thereby to pay homage to Mozart's genius.

ALBI ROSENTHAL

DESCRIPTION OF THE MANUSCRIPT

Size, structure, and layout

M O Z A R T ' S *Thematic Catalogue* has been preserved in good condition for nearly two centuries since his death. The leaves are not entirely rectangular. Their height at the inner margins is 210 mm, and at the outer margins 214 mm; their width varies between approximately 163 and 165 mm. The original binding, which is also well preserved, is a little larger, with a height of 219 mm at the centre and 223 mm at the edges; its width is 170 mm. The volume was produced from 24 bifolia (making 48 leaves); there are six gatherings of four bifolia. But since both the first two and the last two of the 48 leaves were stuck down as end-papers for the binding, there were only 44 leaves conveniently available for Mozart's entries. A diagram of the volume's structure is given in fig.3. The four leaves used as end-papers are listed in the diagram as A, B, C, and D. The first leaf with entries by Mozart (on its verso) was not foliated by him, so it has been given the number 0.

Fig.4 shows the two features of the paper's watermark — a unicorn, and apparently the three letters J.H.I., which are probably the initials of the paper-manufacturer.[1]

Mozart used the majority of the openings of the volume to record his compositions in the following way. On the left-hand page of an opening (the verso of a leaf) he would make five entries, recording the dates of almost always five compositions, followed by the titles of the works, and

---

1 For a similar watermark, cf. Georg Eineder, *The Ancient Paper-Mills of the Former Austro-Hungarian Empire and their Watermarks,* Hilversum, 1960 (Monumenta Chartæ Papyraceæ Historiam Illustrantia, Vol.VIII), No.1691 on Plate 439. Yet the manuscript that contains that watermark is said to be of 1802.

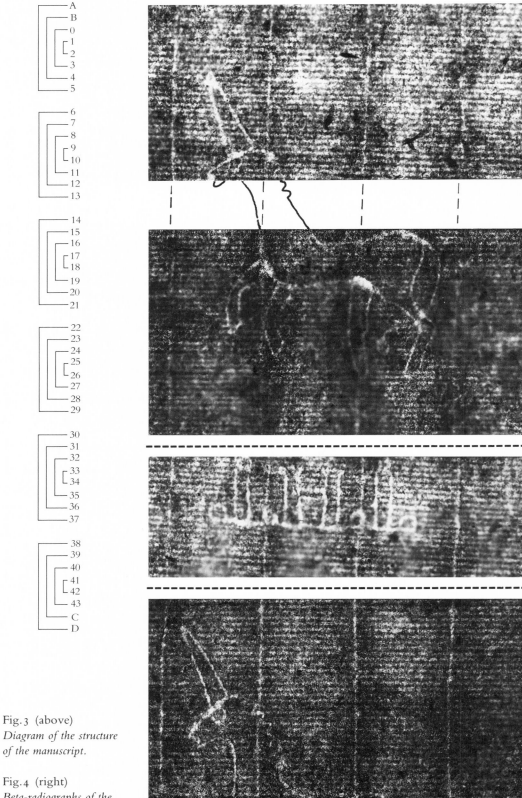

Fig. 3 (above)
Diagram of the structure of the manuscript.

Fig. 4 (right)
Beta-radiographs of the watermarks.

usually their instrumentation too; in the case of operas, and some other vocal compositions, he would add the names of the singers for whom they were written. The facing page of the opening, on the right side (the recto of the next leaf) was ruled with ten staves (five pairs of two staves), which he used for writing the incipits (the opening bars of the music) for the compositions described opposite.

He wrote a folio number at the top of many of the incipit pages; so this pattern has been used for our numbering of the folios. Mozart's numbers are at the tops of the rectos of ff. 1–24, in ink; someone else has numbered ff. 25–28 in pencil. Folio 29, the last one used by Mozart, is unnumbered, as are the unused ff. 30–43 (all of which have been ruled with staves).

Marks and numbers

In addition to what Mozart himself wrote — the dates, descriptions of the compositions, and their incipits on the opposite pages, and the numbers at the tops of ff. 1^r to 24^r — there are many peculiar small entries in the catalogue that were not made by him; they seem to have been added by some of those who had access to the catalogue over many years after his death. These include Constanze Mozart, Georg Nikolaus Nissen (her second husband), the Abbé Maximilian Stadler, Johann Anton André (the purchaser of most of Mozart's autograph scores), André's sons, his assistant Franz Gleissner, and perhaps others. To the left of many of Mozart's descriptive entries there are three small crosses in black ink (or, very occasionally, three short curved lines); above the right-hand end of many incipits there are large crosses in a slightly browner ink; and there are often numbers in roughly the same position, more or less over every fourth incipit, written in a reddish-brown ink. Although the exact meaning of these entries is not clear, it seems probable that some of the crosses were intended to indicate that an autograph score was then extant. If this is the case it is likely that these entries were made by Nissen and/or by André.

There is an obvious significance in another series of numbers; these occur on the left of Mozart's descriptions, and they form a numeration of the items in the catalogue. The very first numbers, 1–5 on f. 0^v, and 6–10 on f. 1^v, are in a dark ink; it is often claimed that they were written by Mozart, but this does not seem to be true since the forms of the numbers are not characteristic of his hand. They may have been inserted by Nissen.

The numbers from 11 onwards are in pencil and were certainly not written by Mozart. They are accurate up to No. 30 on f. 5^v; but No. 30 is repeated beside the first entry on f. 6^v, so that all the pencilled numbers from this page to f. 28^v (the last entries) are too low by one. This has been corrected in the transcription of the entries printed on pp. 35–57, so that when a pencilled number is observed at the left of any descriptive entry from f. 6^v to f. 28^v in the facsimile, the number should be increased by one in order to locate the work in the transcriptions.

Mozart's entries

Let us now consider Mozart's entries, and some of the puzzles associated with them. His description of the *Catalogue*'s contents is in the label on its front cover, which reads:

> Verzeichnüss
> aller meiner Werke
> vom Monath febrario 1784 bis Monath   1
>
> Wolfgang Amadé Mozart [2]

['Catalogue of all my works from the month of February 1784 until the month of   1   .']

Although Mozart died in December 1791, it has been suggested that by writing (after the space left for the month) the figure '1' for the year of the anticipated final entry, rather than '17 ', he expected to be using this volume in 1800, or even later. Yet this strikes some people today as unlikely, in view of his continuous productivity; for from February 1784 until November 1791 he wrote incipits (a few for more than one work) on 145 pairs of staves, and at his death there were only 70 pairs of staves still unused, as one can see in this facsimile.

The very first entry in the *Catalogue* is for the E-flat piano concerto K. 449, with the date of '1784, den 9 ^{ten} Hornung' [= 9 February 1784]. It has usually been assumed that this was approximately the date at which Mozart started to make entries in the *Catalogue*. But an alternative

---

2 The flourish which follows Mozart's signature here has been taken to be an abbreviation 'mpia', meaning 'manu propria' (Latin for 'in my own hand').

14

suggestion has been offered;[3] it has been claimed that there are certain inaccurate features about the dates given to most of the first ten works, and that suggests that they were not written in the *Catalogue* at the exact times of their dates, but were all entered later at more or less the same time, probably in about November 1784. This has also been linked with a serious illness that Mozart developed on 23 August, which lasted for at least three weeks, and his acceptance of apprenticeship in the masonic order on about 7 November. The latter may have been a response to his illness; and was the start of his *Catalogue* perhaps a second response?

Although the first ten entries are in an ink of a similar dark colour (though the date for No.5 is somewhat lighter), the claim that they were all written at about the same time, and given numbers by Mozart, cannot be accepted. For the following ten entries (Nos.11–20), and even all the entries up to No.35 on f.6ᵛ, also look as if they have been made with the same ink and the same writing instrument. Moreover, as has been stated, the argument that the first ten entries were all numbered in Mozart's hand seems unsound. And throughout the *Catalogue,* as shall be explained, works were sometimes entered with dates that did not precisely correspond to the time that they were finished. So it is indeed quite possible that he really started his *Catalogue* in February 1784.

Three entries at the bottom of ff.19ᵛ, 20ᵛ and 23ᵛ are not numbered; they list the four vocal works by Handel that Mozart rescored for performances in Vienna, and these entries he marked 'NB:'. They were obviously added somewhat later than the other entries on those pages; possibly they were all written at the same time, together with the second work, K.587, prefixed by 'NB', in No.117 on f.23ᵛ, with its incipit on f.24ʳ. None of the Handel entries has an incipit on the facing page.

Lost compositions

There are a few entries for compositions that seem not to have survived in any form. Mozart has provided a description of each of these works and usually of its scoring, the date at which it was finished, and its incipit. It

---

3   Cf. Daniel N. Leeson & David Whitwell, 'Mozart's Thematic Catalogue', *The Musical Times*, Vol.114 (1973), pp.781–783.

is always possible that an autograph, or at least a copyist's score, of any of them could be discovered one day, but after two centuries this must now be unlikely. However, they were included in Köchel's numbering. The works in question are:

No. 19	K. 470: Andante for a violin concerto (1 April 1785).
No. 65	K. 525: 1st minuet and trio of Eine kleine Nachtmusik (10 August 1787). It was almost certainly on the now missing f. 3 of the autograph. There is no incipit for this movement.
No. 86	K. 544: Little march (26 June 1788).
No. 99	K. 565: Two contredanses for eight instruments (30 October 1788).
No. 102	K. 569: Aria for soprano(?), 'Ohne Zwang . . .' (January 1789).
No. 136	K. 615: Final chorus to an opera by Giuseppe Sarti (20 April 1791).

Omissions from the Catalogue

The description in the label on the front cover of the *Catalogue* seems to imply Mozart's intention to include descriptions and dates for all the compositions finished from February 1784 up to the last months of his life. In consequence of this, nearly all the Köchel numbers from 449 to 623 have been given to the entered works. Many works that are not in the *Catalogue* were assumed to have been composed before February 1784, and they were consequently given Köchel numbers below 449.

But in more recent times it has often been suggested that Mozart omitted from the *Catalogue* quite a large number of the compositions that he wrote on various occasions within the period it covers. Lists of about 20 such works have been produced; but it is by no means certain that all of them were unintentionally overlooked by Mozart.

He may perhaps have regarded his *Catalogue* as primarily a list of the works that he could arrange to have publicly performed, either under his own supervision or by passing them to other musicians; and possibly also entries for the very few works that he had hopes of getting published. There are, of course, many other entries that do not fall into these categories. Yet he might not have bothered to enter one or two works written for a 'private' family performance, or for special social occasions, or for an unusual soloist (i.e. a work that could not be performed by anyone else). This might help to explain some of Mozart's omissions, even though many of his compositions of these types *were* included. The following list is of some of the works omitted by Mozart from the *Catalogue*.

K.298   Quartet for flute, violin, viola, and violoncello. This was not written in Paris in 1778, as Köchel claimed, but in Vienna at the end of 1787.

K.355(576b) Minuet in D for piano, probably written in about 1789–90; it was published in 1801 with a Trio composed by the Abbé Maximilian Stadler.

K.356(617a) Adagio for harmonica, probably written in the first half of 1791.

K.406(516b) String Quintet in C minor, arranged from the wind serenade that he wrote in 1782, K.388(384a). The string quintet was probably finished early in 1788.

K.436, K.437, K.438, K.439, K.346(439a) Five Notturni for two sopranos and a bass. They were not written in 1783 (or in one case even earlier) as Köchel claimed, but in about 1787 or later.

K.441   'Das Bandel', for soprano, tenor, and bass, and string-quartet accompaniment. Not written in 1783, as Köchel claimed, but in about 1786 or 1787.

K.447   Horn Concerto in E flat. Not written in 1783, as Köchel claimed, but in about 1787. [*See* fig. 5.]

K.453a   Little Funeral March for piano (16 bars), written as an entry in Barbara Ployer's album. It is however possible that this piece was written before February 1784, in spite of the fact that the first and the fifth works entered in the *Catalogue*, the piano concertos K.449 and K.453, were also written for her.

K.469   The cantata *Davidde penitente,* largely based on the music for the Mass in C minor, K.427(417a), was first performed on 13 March 1785. Although Mozart did not enter the whole work in the catalogue, he entered the two new arias that he wrote for it, K.469, no.6 (6 March) and no.8 (11 March).

K.483	'Zerfliesset heut', geliebte Brüder', masonic song, with male chorus. Written probably at the end of 1785, or in 1786.
K.484	'Ihr unsre neuen Leiter', masonic song, with male chorus. Written probably at the end of 1785, or in 1786.
K.485	Rondo in D for piano. The autograph score is dated by Mozart '10 January 1786'.
K.487(496a)	12 Duos for two horns. The partial autograph score (with only nos. 3, 1, and 6) is dated by Mozart '27 July 1786'.
K.506	'Lied der Freiheit', a song published in the *Wiener Musenalmanach* for 1786. That volume was out by January 1786, so the song was probably written in 1785.
K.579	'Un moto di gioia', an aria for Susanna in the revival of *Le nozze di Figaro* at Vienna in August 1789.
K.621a(Anh.245)	'Io ti lascio', aria for bass, often dated 'September 1791 in Prague', but perhaps a little earlier — e.g. early 1788, after Mozart's return from Prague at the end of 1787.

Although it is hard to explain most of these omissions, some suggestions can be put forward. The Notturni K.436, K.437, K.438, K.439, and K.346(439a) were perhaps written purely for performance by his friends, such as Gottfried von Jacquin. The same seems to apply to 'Das Bandel', K.441, 'for Constanze, Mozart and Jacquin', and K.621a, which was also perhaps written for von Jacquin. (Yet Mozart did enter K.513, and described it as 'an aria for Gottfried von Jacquin'.) K.447 was another work written for performance by a friend, Ignaz Leutgeb, the horn-player for whom Mozart wrote most of his horn works. (Yet another horn concerto for Leutgeb, K.495, *was* entered in the catalogue.) Because K.453a was merely a little work of 16 bars in Barbara Ployer's album, Mozart probably did not think it suitable for inclusion in the catalogue, though he did enter the more considerable 'kleine Gigue', K.574, which he wrote in the album of Karl Immanuel Engel, an organist at Leipzig.

K.483 and K.484, two songs with accompaniments for chorus and organ, were probably written just for performance together at a masonic celebration.

Although Susanna's new aria 'Un moto do gioia', K.579, written for the August 1789 revival of *Le nozze di Figaro* at Vienna, was omitted from

Fig. 5 *Opening of Mozart's autograph manuscript of K.447, Horn Concerto in E Flat. British Library, Stefan Zweig MS 55, f.1.*

the catalogue, her other new aria, the rondò 'Al desio, di chi t'adora', K.577, *was* entered. This inconsistency is hard to understand.

The rondo for piano, K.485, was perhaps a composition written merely for teaching purposes. If so, this could possibly explain its omission.

Even when quite a large part of a work had been written, Mozart would not enter it until he regarded it as finished. Thus many fragmentary pieces on which he worked during the years of the *Catalogue*, and of course the unfinished *Requiem*, K.626, are not entered in it.

Yet he entered one or two songs, autographs of which have slightly incomplete piano accompaniments. No doubt Mozart considered them as finished, for he will have had no difficulty in playing them.

Inaccuracies in the entries

However, it is clear that Mozart did not fail to enter the great majority of the compositions that he completed between February 1784 and the time of his death in 1791. This is why the *Catalogue* is so valuable, especially because of the dates that he gave to almost every work, his helpful descriptions of them all, their instrumentation, sometimes the names of the singers or instrumentalists for whom they were written, and the incipits.

Yet it is nevertheless the case that there are a few inaccuracies in some of his entries Not that features such as his spelling mistakes, or his inconsistent version of the opening words of an aria or a song, cause any trouble. For instance, the heading at the beginning of the song 'Das Alte', K.517, 'Ein bißchen aus der Nase', was entered in the incipit as 'Ein bißchen durch die Nase'. The song entitled 'Das Traumbild', K.530, was entered as 'das Traumlied'. The opening words of the duet 'Per queste tue manine', K.540b, added to the May 1788 Vienna version of *Don Giovanni,* were entered as 'Per quelle tue Manine'. And the opening words of the bass aria 'Rivolgete a lui lo sguardo', K.584, were entered as 'Rivolgete à me lo sguardo'.

More puzzling are a few of the tempi in the incipits, since they differ from those in the autograph scores. Here are some of the most striking ones, the *Catalogue*'s entry being cited first:

No.17	K.469, no.8: Larghetto, instead of Andante.
No.18	K.468: Andantino, instead of Larghetto.
No.34	K.489: Andante, instead of Larghetto.
No.37	K.492: Overture: Allegro assai, instead of Presto.
No.40	K.495: Allegro, instead of Allegro moderato.
No.67	K.527: Overture (D-major entry): Allegro assai, instead of Molto allegro.
No.107	K.575: Allegro, instead of Allegretto. [*See* fig.6.]
No.118	K.588: Overture: Andante Maestoso, instead of Andante.
No.121	K.593: Adagio, instead of Larghetto.
No.138	K.617: the Rondo: Allegro, instead of Allegretto.

These divergences may be used as evidence that Mozart did not draw much of a distinction between the use of a few of these tempi.

Fig.6 *Opening of Mozart's autograph manuscript of K.575, String Quartet in D. British Library, Additional MS 37765, f.1ʳ.*

Some of the entries give a work slightly different orchestration from what is regarded as the true form, or the version in the autograph. In some cases it may be that Mozart did not make an error in the *Catalogue*, but later changed a composition's scoring. Here are some examples:

No.11   K.459. The '2 Clarini, timpany' are not in the autograph.

No.26   K.477(479a). This work's Kontrafagott is not included, and only one of its three basset-horns is mentioned.

No.74   K.535. '2 oboe' are listed instead of the autograph's two clarinets.

In No. 75, K. 536, No. 101, K. 568, and No. 104, K. 571, there is no mention in the *Catalogue* of the two horns which are apparently part of their scoring.

Another possible change that Mozart may have made to a composition, K. 573, is the number of variations for piano on a minuet by Jean Pierre Duport. For his entry, No. 105 (dated '29 April 1789 in Potsdam'), describes it as having six variations, but today we have nine. In August 1791 the Viennese copyist–publisher Laurent Lausch advertised it for sale as '6 variations', but at about the same time the Berlin and Amsterdam publisher J.J. Hummel produced an edition of nine variations. So perhaps Mozart augmented this work after making his entry in the *Catalogue*.

Although Mozart's dates in the *Catalogue* are mostly regarded as being reliable, there are one or two that are somewhat puzzling. No. 26, K. 477(479a) is dated July 1785. The title of this C-minor orchestral work is 'Maurerische Trauermusik' — that is, masonic funeral music; and the catalogue's entry declares that it was for the deaths of the Duke Georg August von Mecklenburg-Strelitz and of the Count Franz Esterházy von Galantha. However, they had not died in the summer of 1785, but on 6 and 7 November. So when Mozart entered this work, which cannot have been before November 1785, it seems possible that he overlooked the fact that the words 'im Monath Jully' had perhaps already been entered at the top of the page, f. 5ᵛ; for the previous entry, at the bottom of f. 4ᵛ, is dated 8 June. According to a recent suggestion, Mozart had an earlier version of this work, incorporating vocal parts, performed at a masonic ceremony on 12 August 1785; so it is claimed that this resulted in a faulty early date for the orchestral composition produced in November 1785.[4]

The very next work in the *Catalogue*, No. 27, K. 478, the G-minor piano quartet, seems also to be misdated. For it is assigned the same date as the masonic funeral music, the word 'detto' implying July 1785. Yet the autograph of K. 478 is dated 16 October 1785, and it seems very likely that this was when it was completed.

Although No. 16, K. 467, a C-major piano concerto, is dated 9 March 1785 in the *Catalogue*, the autograph has a very slightly earlier date: February 1785. Here it is hard to say which is more accurate.

In some cases Mozart may have finished a composition, and perhaps had

---

4   Cf. Philippe A. Autexier, 'Wann wurde die Maurerische Trauermusik uraufgeführt?', *Mozart-Jahrbuch 1984/85*, pp. 6–8.

Fig.7   *Mozart's autograph manuscript of the fifth of the contredanses, K.609.*
British Library, Stefan Zweig MS 59, f.3″.

it performed, but later decided to change it in some way, and possibly even to rescore it. So he may then have entered the work in his *Catalogue* at a rather later date than the one suggested by some of the surviving source material. Here are two examples.

The *Catalogue*'s date for No.7, K.455, ten variations for piano on 'Unser dummer Pöbel meint', a melody from a Singspiel by Christoph Willibald Gluck, is 25 August 1784. Since it is known that Mozart had played variations on this theme at a concert in Vienna on 23 March 1783, at which Gluck was probably in the audience, the *Catalogue*'s date has sometimes been regarded as inaccurate. But although we have a fragmentary autograph of about 4½ variations, which almost certainly dates from 1783, we also have an autograph of all the ten variations, which probably dates from 1784. No doubt Mozart wrote this in preparation for the work's publication, which possibly took place in 1785, or certainly no later than 1786.

It seems very probable that he wrote the soprano aria 'Ah se in ciel, benigne stelle' in 1778 for the lady he was then very devoted to, Aloysia Weber, the sister of his future wife Constanze.[5] But the final autograph of the aria is dated 4 March 1788 and is inscribed 'per la Sig:^{ra} Lange', the married name of Aloysia. And the entry in the *Catalogue*, No. 77, K. 538, has the same date and inscription as the final autograph.

Some other difficulties of this kind are probably to be explained by Mozart's official appointment in December 1787 as 'Kammermusikus', chamber music composer for the Imperial and Royal Court. As he was expected regularly to supply collections of dance music for court balls, he appears to have revised, or rescored, earlier pieces and often entered them in new groupings. For example, No. 132 in the *Catalogue* includes two works dated 6 March 1791: K. 610, a Contredanse in G, and K. 611, a German dance in C. Yet K. 611, with slightly different scoring, is also the third of the four German dances K. 602, entered as half of No. 127, dated 5 February 1791. And K. 610, with slightly different scoring, is also the fifth of the five contredanses K. 609, a collection not entered in the *Catalogue*, but given the proposed date of 1791 by Köchel. Moreover the autograph of K. 609's five contredanses (*see* fig. 7), although not dated, appears to have been written in 1787 or 1788; and the second autograph of K. 610 (alone), also not dated, appears to have been written much earlier, probably in about 1783.[6] By the assumption that these were works that Mozart revised in various ways for the court balls, the problems in some of the information provided by the *Catalogue* can often be solved.

ALAN TYSON

---

5   There is an autograph with merely the voice part and the bass line, which seems to have been written near the end of 1778. Cf. Alan Tyson, *Mozart: Studies of the Autograph Scores*, Cambridge, Mass: Harvard U.P., 1987, pp. 232–233.

6   Since this autograph gives the work the title of 'Les filles malicieuses', it would appear that it had not been written for the court.

Mozart's *Catalogue*, as has been shown, poses many questions for scholars, some of which will probably never be answered. Nevertheless the transcriptions and facsimile pages that follow will give a wider public the opportunity to study these questions for themselves, perhaps to pose new questions, and to draw new conclusions. The work of interpretation will continue, but the *Catalogue* remains an unparalleled record of the working life of one of the greatest composers of all time and a vital source for an understanding of his development.

TRANSCRIPTIONS OF MOZART'S ENTRIES

On the following pages there are transcriptions of all Mozart's *Catalogue* entries, and at the foot of each page brief notes to help the reader to identify each of the listed works.

The entries have been numbered here in their order, from [1] to [145], except that Mozart's three entries (without incipits) listing four works by Handel that he had rescored are not numbered. As for the numbers contained in the *Catalogue*, it now seems clear that Mozart did not write even the first ten, which are in ink; these ten, and all the other ones, which are in pencil, were added by later hands. The numbers printed here correspond to those added by these other hands up to No.[30]. Because of their error in numbering two separate entries both '30' (*see* p.14 above), our numbers from f.6ᵛ onwards are one figure higher than the pencil numbers that can often be seen in the facsimile. The K. numbers identifying the works are taken from the sixth edition (1964) of Köchel's catalogue, though in fact only a few vary from those to be found in the first edition (1862).

For his entries Mozart uses two styles of handwriting, with different forms for many letters: 'German script', and 'Roman script'. He used the former for most of the German-language entries, and the latter for most of the Italian words. Very often he does not use a capital letter for the beginning of a German noun (e.g. 'klavier', & 'lied'); and many Italian nouns, such as the names of instruments, usually have lower-case letters, but occasionally capitals. It is frequently not clear whether the letter that he wrote is intended to be a capital or not. These ambiguities can be seen in the facsimile.

There are occasional errors in Mozart's spelling. He misspells a few proper names, and some other words. In No.[117], where Mozart wrote 'ai nedemi istromenti', he should have written 'ai medesimi istromenti'.

In Italian plural nouns and proper names ending in 'i', although Mozart often writes 'fagotti' and 'clarinetti', he also often carries down the stroke of the final letter to a greater or lesser degree, so that it may be a 'j'. But even if he may sometimes write 'fagottj' or 'clarinettj', the transcriptions here print the last letter as 'i'. These deviations can be seen in the facsimile. One can also see in the facsimile some entries like ' *c* :'. This is the way in which Mozart abbreviates 'et cetera'; here it is transcribed as 'etc.'.

1784.

den 9 ᵗᵉⁿ Hornung.

[1]   *Ein klavierkonzert. begleitung. 2 violini, viola e Baßo. –(2 oboe, 2 corni ad libitum.)*

den 15 ᵗᵉⁿ März.

[2]   *Ein klavier konzert. begleitung. 2 violini, 2 viole, 1 flauto, 2 oboe, 2 fagotti, 2 Corni e Baßo.*

den 22 ᵗᵉⁿ

[3]   *Ein klavierkonzert. begleitung. 2 violini, 2 viole, 1 flauto, 2 oboe, 2 fagotti, 2 corni, 2 clarini, timpany e Baßo.*

den 30 ᵗᵉⁿ

[4]   *Ein klavier Quintett. begleitung. 1 oboe, 1 clarinetto, 1 corno, et 1 fagotto.*

den 12 ᵗᵉⁿ Aprill.

[5]   *Ein klavier konzert. begleitung. 2 violini, 2 viole, 1 flauto, 2 oboe, 2 fagotti, 2 corni, e Baßo.*

---

[1]   K.449 Piano concerto in E flat.

[2]   K.450 Piano concerto in B flat.

[3]   K.451 Piano concerto in D.

[4]   K.452 Quintet in E flat for piano, oboe, clarinet, horn, and bassoon.

[5]   K.453 Piano concerto in G.

den 21 ! Aprill.

[6]   *Eine klavier Sonate mit einer Violin.*

den 25 ! August.

[7]   *10 Variazionen für das klavier allein.*

den 30 ! September.

[8]   *Ein klavier konzert. begleitung. 2 violini, 2 viole, 1 flauto, 2 oboe, 2 fagotti,*
        2 Corni e Baßo.

den 14 ᵗᵉⁿ oktober.

[9]   *Eine Sonate für das klavier allein.*

den 9 ᵗᵉⁿ November.

[10]   *Ein Quartett für 2 violini, viola e violoncello.*

---

[6]   K.454 Sonata in B flat for piano and violin.

[7]   K.455 Ten variations for piano on a song by Gluck, 'Unser dummer Pöbel meint'.

[8]   K.456 Piano concerto in B flat.

[9]   K.457 Piano sonata in C minor.

[10]   K.458 String quartet in B flat, often called the 'Hunt' quartet (published as the third of the
        'Haydn' quartets, but the fourth to be finished).

den 11 ͭᵉⁿ december.

[11] *Ein klavier konzert. begleitung. 2 violini, 2 viole, 1 flauto, 2 oboe, 2 fagotti,*
         2 Corni, 2 Clarini, timpany e Baßo.

                                    1785.
                        den 10 ͭᵉⁿ Jenner.

[12] *Ein Quartett für 2 violini, viola e violoncello.*

                        den 14 ͭᵉⁿ

[13] *Ein Quartett für 2 violini, viola e Violoncello.*

                        den 10 ͭᵉⁿ Hornung.

[14] *Ein klavier konzert. Begleitung. 2 violini, 2 viole, 1 flauto, 2 oboe,*
         2 fagotti, 2 Corni, 2 Clarini, timpany e Baßo.

                        den 6 ͭᵉⁿ März.

[15] *Eine Arie für Adamberger zur SocietätsMusique. À te frà tanti affanni etc:*
         begleitung. 2 violini, 2 viole, 1 flauto, 1 oboe, 1 clarinetto, 1 fagotti, 2 Corni e Baßo.

---

[11]   K.459 Piano concerto in F.

[12]   K.464 String quartet in A (the fifth of the 'Haydn' quartets).

[13]   K.465 String quartet in C (the sixth of the 'Haydn' quartets).

[14]   K.466 Piano concerto in D minor.

[15]   K.469, No.6 Aria, 'A te, fra tanti affanni', for the cantata *Davidde penitente*.

den 9 ᵗᵉⁿ: März.

[16] *Ein klavier konzert. Begleitung. 2 violini, 2 Viole, 1 flauto, 2 oboe, 2 fagotti,*
 2 Corni, 2 Clarini, timpany e Baßo.

den 11 ᵗᵉⁿ:

[17] *Ein Arie für die Cavaglieri zur SocietätsMusique. – Tra l'oscure ombre funeste etc:*
 Begleitung. 2 violini, 2 viole, 1 flauto, 2 oboe, 2 fagotti, 2 Corni e Baßo.

den 26 ᵗᵉⁿ:

[18] *MaurerGesellen=lied für Singstiͫe und klavier. Die ihr einem Neuen Grade*
 der Erkeͫtnüss nun euch naht etc:

den 1 ᵗᵉⁿ: Aprill.

[19] *Ein Andante für die Violin zu einen konzert. Begleitung. 2 Violini, Viola,*
 2 oboe, 2 Corni e Baßo.

den 20 ᵗᵉⁿ:

[20] *Eine kleine kantate. Die Maurerfreude. — Singstiͫe. Tenor. und zum*
 Schluß ein kleiner Chor von 2 tenor und 1ⁿᵉᵐ Baß. Begleitung. 2 violini,
 2 viole, 1 clarinetto, 2 oboe, 2 Corni e Baßo.

---

[16] K.467 Piano concerto in C.

[17] K.469, No.8 Aria, 'Fra l'oscure ombre funeste', for the cantata *Davidde penitente*.

[18] K.468 Masonic song with piano accompaniment, *Gesellenreise*.

[19] K.470 Andante in A for a violin concerto. (This work is lost).

[20] K.471 Masonic cantata for tenor and chorus with a small orchestral accompaniment, 'Sehen,
 wie dem starren Forscherauge'.

den 7 ͭᵉⁿ May.

[21]   *Ein lied für klavier und Singstime. der Zauberer.*

detto.

[22]   *Ein lied. ————————— die Zufriedenheit.*

detto.

[23]   *Ein lied. ————— die Betrogene Welt.*

den 20 ͭᵉⁿ

[24]   *Eine Phantasie für das klavier allein.*

den 8 ͭᵉⁿ Juny.

[25]   *Ein lied für klavier und Singstime. ————— das Veilchen.*

---

[21]   K.472 Song with piano accompaniment, *Der Zauberer.*

[22]   K.473 Song with piano accompaniment, *Die Zufriedenheit.*

[23]   K.474 Song with piano accompaniment, *Die betrogene Welt.*

[24]   K.475 Fantasia in C minor for piano, published together with the piano sonata in C minor, K.457, No.[9] above.

[25]   K.476 Song with piano accompaniment, *Das Veilchen.*

im Monath Jully.

[26] *Maurerische TrauerMusick bey dem Todfalle der Brbr: Meklenburg und Esterhazy. — 2 violini, 2 viole, 1 Clarinett, 1 Baßethorn, 2 oboe, 2 Corni e Baßo.*

detto.

[27] *Ein Quartett für klavier, 1 Violin, 1 Viola und Violoncello.*

den 5 ᵗᵉⁿ November.

[28] *Quartetto in die oper. La villanella rapita. für Sigᵘ Coltellini, Sigᵉ Calvesi, Sigᵉ Mandini e Bußani. begleitung. 2 violini, 2 viole, 2 oboe, 2 Clarinetti, 2 fagotti, 2 Corni e Baßo.*

den 21 ᵗᵉⁿ

[29] *Tarzetto in detta opera. für Sigᵘ Coltellini, Sigᵉ Calvesi e Mandini. Begleitung. 2 violini, 2 viole, 2 flauti, 2 oboe, 2 clarinetti, 2 fagotti, 2 Corni e Baßo.*

den 12 ᵗᵉⁿ December.

[30] *Eine klavier Sonate mit begleitung einer Violin.*

---

[26] K.477(479a) Masonic funeral music in C minor for orchestra.

[27] K.478 Quartet in G minor for piano, violin, viola, and violoncello.

[28] K.479 Quartet for soprano, tenor, and two basses, with orchestral accompaniment, 'Dite almeno, in che mancai', for inclusion in the opera *La villanella rapita* by Francesco Bianchi.

[29] K.480 Trio for soprano, tenor, and bass, with orchestral accompaniment, 'Mandina amabile', for inclusion in *La villanella rapita*.

[30] K.481 Sonata for piano and violin in E flat.

34

den 16 ^{ten}. december.

[31] *Ein klavierkonzert. begleitung. 2 Violini, 2 Viole, 1 flauto, 2 clarinetti,*
  2 fagotti, 2 Corni, 2 clarini, timpani e Baßo.

1786.

den 3 ^{ten}. Hornung.

[32] *Der SchauspielDirektor. Eine komödie mit Musick für Schönbrun. bestehend aus Ouverture,*
  2 Arien, ein Terzett und Vaudeville. — für Mad:^{me} Lange, Mad^{selle}: Cavaglieri,
  und M^r: Adamberger.

den 2 ^{ten}. März.

[33] *Ein klavier konzert. Begleitung. 2 violini, 2 viole, 1 flauto, 2 Clarinetti,*
  2 fagotti, 2 Corni e Baßo.

den 10 ^{ten}.

[34] *Ein Duetto zu meiner oper Idomeneo. für die fr: von Puffendorf und Bar: Pulini.*
  begleitung. 2 violini, 2 viole, 2 oboe, 2 fagotti, 2 Corni e Baßo.

detto.

[35] *Scena con Rondò mit violin solo für Bar: Pulini und Graf Hatzfeldt in*
  die obenbemeldte oper. begleitung. 2 violini, 2 viole, 2 clarinetti,
  2 fagotti, 2 Corni e Baßo.

---

[31] K.482 Piano concerto in E flat.

[32] K.486 *Der Schauspieldirektor*, comedy with music in one act, first performed in Vienna on
  7 February 1786.

[33] K.488 Piano concerto in A.

[34] K.489 Duet for soprano and tenor, 'Spiegarti non poss'io', for a private performance of a
  revised version of *Idomeneo* on 13 March 1786.

[35] K.490 Scena with Rondò for tenor, with violin solo, 'Non più, tutto ascoltai' and 'Non
  temer, amato bene', for a private performance of a revised version of *Idomeneo*
  on 13 March 1786.

den 24 ᵗᵉⁿ: März.

[36] *Ein klavier konzert. Begleitung. 2 violini, 2 viole, 1 flauto, 2 oboe,*
2 clarinetti, 2 fagotti, 2 corni, 2 clarini, timpany e Baßo.

den 29 ᵗᵉⁿ: Aprill.

[37] *Le Nozze di figaro. opera buffa. in 4 Atti. — Pezzi di Musica. 34. Attori.*
Signore. storace, laschi, mandini, Bußani, e Nañina gottlieb. — Sig:ʳⁱ Benucci,
mandini, occhely, e Bußani. —

den 3 ᵗᵉⁿ: Juny.

[38] *Ein Quartett für klavier, violin, viola und violoncello.*

den 10 ᵗᵉⁿ:

[39] *Ein kleines Rondò für das klavier allein.*

den 26 ᵗᵉⁿ:

[40] *Ein Waldhorn konzert für den Leitgeb. begleitung. 2 violini, 2 viole,*
2 oboe, 2 Corni e Baßo.

---

[36] K.491 Piano concerto in C minor.

[37] K.492 *Le Nozze di Figaro* ('The Marriage of Figaro'), comic opera in 4 acts, first performed
in Vienna on 1 May 1786.

[38] K.493 Quartet in E flat for piano, violin, viola, and violoncello.

[39] K.494 Rondo in F for piano, eventually used as the finale of a piano sonata, for which
K.533, No.[72] below, provided the first two movements.

[40] K.495 Horn concerto in E flat.

den 8 ᵗᵉⁿ Jully.

[41]   *Ein terzett für klavier, violin und Violoncello.*

den 1 ᵗᵉⁿ August.

[42]   *Ein klavier Sonate auf 4 Hände.*

den 5 ᵗᵉⁿ

[43]   *Ein Terzett für klavier, Clarinett und Viola.*

den 19 ᵗᵉⁿ

[44]   *Ein Quartett für 2 violin, viola und Violoncello.*

den 12 ᵗᵉⁿ September.

[45]   *12 variazionen für das klavier allein.*

---

[41]   K.496 Trio in G for piano, violin, and violoncello.

[42]   K.497 Piano sonata in F for four hands.

[43]   K.498 Trio in E flat for piano, clarinet, and viola.

[44]   K.499 String quartet in D, often called the 'Hoffmeister' quartet, the name of its publisher.

[45]   K.500 Twelve variations for piano, perhaps on an original theme.

den 4 ͭᵉⁿ November.

[46] *Variazionen für das klavier. auf 4 Hände.*

den 18 ͭᵉⁿ

[47] *Ein Terzett für klavier, violin und Violoncello.*

den 4 ͭᵉⁿ december

[48] *Ein klavier konzert. Begleitung. 2 violini, 2 viole, 1 flauto, 2 oboe,*
       2 fagotti, 2 Corni, 2 Clarini, timpany e Baßo.

den 6 ͭᵉⁿ

[49] *Eine Sinfonie. — 2 violini, 2 viole, 2 flauti, 2 oboe, 2 Corni, 2 fagotti*
       2 clarini, timpany e Baßo.

den 27 ͭᵉⁿ

[50] *Scena con Rondò mit klavier solo. für Mad ˢᵉˡˡᵉ storace und mich. begleitung. 2 violini,*
       2 viole, 2 clarinetti, 2 fagotti, 2 corni e Baßo.

---

[46] K.501 Five variations for piano, for four hands.

[47] K.502 Trio in B flat for piano, violin, and violoncello.

[48] K.503 Piano concerto in C.

[49] K.504 Symphony in D, often called the 'Prague' symphony.

[50] K.505 Scena, 'Ch'io mi scordi di te', and Rondò, 'Non temer, amato bene', for soprano and
       piano, with orchestra.

1787.

in Prag

den 6 ᵗᵉⁿ febrario.

[51] *6 Teutsche. 2 violini, 2 flauti, 1 flauto piccolo; 2 oboe, 2 clarinetti, 2 fagotti,*
     2 Corni, 2 clarini, timpany e Baßo.

Wieñ.

den 11 ᵗᵉⁿ März.

[52] *Ein Rondò für das klavier allein.*

den 18 ᵗᵉⁿ

[53] *Scena für H: fischer. non sò d'onde viene etc: begleitung. 2 Violini, 2 viole,*
     1 flauto, 2 oboe, 2 fagotti, 2 Corni e Baßo.

den 23 ᵗᵉⁿ

[54] *Eine Arie für H: Gottfried von Jacquin. Mentre ti lascio o figlia etc:*
     begleitung. 2 violini, 2 viole, 1 flauto, 2 clarinetti, 2 fagotti, 2 Corni e Baßo.

den 19 ᵗᵉⁿ Aprill.

[55] *Ein Quintett für 2 violini, 2 viole und violoncello.*

---

[51] K.509 Six German dances for orchestra.

[52] K.511 Rondo in A minor for piano.

[53] K.512 Recitative, 'Alcandro, lo confesso', and aria, 'Non sò, d'onde viene', for bass with orchestra accompaniment.

[54] K.513 Aria for bass with orchestral accompaniment, 'Mentre ti lascio, o figlia'.

[55] K.515 String quintet in C.

den 16 ᵗᵉⁿ May.

[56] *Ein Quintett für 2 violin, 2 viole und Violoncello.*

den 18 ᵗᵉⁿ

[57] *Ein Lied für klavier und Singstime. die Alte.*

den 20 ᵗᵉⁿ

[58] *Ein lied —— —— die Verschweigung. ——*

den 23 ᵗᵉⁿ

[59] *Ein Lied. — die Trennung.*

den 26 ᵗᵉⁿ

[60] *Ein Lied. —— —— als Luise die briefe ihres ungetreuen liebhabers verbrannte.*

---

[56] K.516 String quintet in G minor.

[57] K.517 Song with piano accompaniment, *Die Alte.*

[58] K.518 Song with piano accompaniment, *Die Verschweigung.*

[59] K.519 Song with piano accompaniment, *Das Lied der Trennung.*

[60] K.520 Song with piano accompaniment, *Als Luise die Briefe . . .*

den 29 ⁱᵉⁿ May.

[61] *Eine klavier Sonate auf vier Hände.*

den 14 ⁱᵉⁿ Juny.

[62] *Ein Musikalischer Spass; bestehend in einem Allegro, Menuett und Trio,*
      Adagio, und finale. — 2 violini, viola, 2 corni, e Baßo.

den 24 ⁱᵉⁿ Juny.

[63] *Ein lied. —— —— AbendEmpfindung.*

detto.

[64] *Ein lied. —— —— An Chloe. ——*

den 10 ⁱᵉⁿ August

[65] *Eine kleine NachtMusick, bestehend in einem Allegro, Menuett*
      und Trio. — Romance. Menuett und Trio, und finale.
      — 2 Violini, Viola e Baßi.

---

[61] K.521 Piano sonata in C for four hands.

[62] K.522 Sextet in F for strings and horns, *Ein musikalischer Spass* (= 'a musical joke').

[63] K.523 Song with piano accompaniment, *Abendempfindung.*

[64] K.524 Song with piano accompaniment, *An Chloe.*

[65] K.525 'Eine kleine Nachtmusik', serenade in G for five strings.

den 24ᵗᵉⁿ

[66] *Eine klavier Sonate mit begleitung einer Violin.*

den 28ᵗᵉⁿ October.
in Prag.

[67] *Il diβoluto punito, o, il Don Giovanni. opera Buffa in 2 Atti. —*
   Pezzi di musica. 24. Attori. Signore. Teresa saporiti, Bondini, e Micelli.
   Signori. Paβi, Ponziani, baglioni e Lolli. —

den 3ᵗᵉⁿ November.

[68] *scena. für Madᵐᵉ Duscheck. Recitativo: — bella mia fiam̄a. — Aria. Resta,*
   O Cara etc: begleitung. —

den 6ᵗᵉⁿ

[69] *Ein lied. —— —— Am Geburtstag des fritzes.*

detto

[70] *Ein lied. —— —— das Traumlied.*

---

[66] K.526 Sonata in A for piano and violin.

[67] K.527 *Don Giovanni* (or *Il dissoluto punito*), comic opera in 2 acts, first performed in Prague on 29 October 1787.

[68] K.528 Dramatic recitative, 'Bella mia fiamma', and aria, 'Resta, o cara', for soprano, with orchestral accompaniment.

[69] K.529 Song with piano accompaniment, *Des kleinen Friedrichs Geburtstag.*

[70] K.530 Song with piano accompaniment, *Das Traumbild.*

den 11 ! dec ᵇʳᵉ.

[71] *Ein lied. — — die kleine Spinnerin. ——*

den 3 ! Jenner. 1788.

[72] *Ein Allegro und Andante für das klavier allein.*

den 14 ! detto.

[73] *Einen Contredanse. Das Donnerwetter. — à 2 violini, 2 oboe,*
      2 Corni, 1 flautino, 1 troͫel, und Baßo.

den 23 ! ——

[74] *Einen Contredanse. die Batallie. — à 2 violini, 2 oboe, 1 flautino,*
      1 Tromba. 1 troͫel e Baßo.

den 27 ! ——

[75] *6 Teutsche. — à 2 violini, 2 flauti, 2 oboe, 2 clarinetti, 2 fagotti, 2 clarini, timpany,*
      flautino, e Baßi. —

---

[71] K.531 Song with piano accompaniment, *Die kleine Spinnerin.*

[72] K.533 Allegro and Andante for piano, used with the Rondo K.494, No.[39], to make a
      piano sonata in F.

[73] K.534 Contredanse called 'Das Donnerwetter', for orchestra.

[74] K.535 Contredanse called 'La Bataille', for orchestra.

[75] K.536 Six German dances for orchestra.

den 24 ! feb:

[76] *Ein klavier konzert in D dur. — à 2 violini, viola e Baßo.*
        1 flauto, 2 oboe, 2 fagotti, 2 Corni, 2 clarini et timpany ad libitum.

den 4 ᵗᵉⁿ März.

[77] *Eine Arie in f dur. — Ah se in ciel benigne stelle etc: für Mad:ᵐᵉ Lange.*
        begleitung. 2 violini, 2 oboe, 2 fagotti, 2 Corni, viola e Baßo.

den 5 ᵗᵉⁿ —

[78] *Ein teutsches kriegs=lied für den Jüngern Bauman, Schauspieler in der Leopolds-Stadt.*
        in A. — Ich möchte wohl der kayser seyn etc: begleitung. 2 violini, 2 oboe, 2 Corni,
        2 fagotti, 1 flauto piccolo. Piatti, Tamburo grande, viole e Baßi. —

den 19 ᵗᵉⁿ —

[79] *Ein Adagio für das klavier allein. in H mol. —*

den 24 ᵗᵉⁿ Aprill.

[80] *Eine Arie zur Oper: Don Giovanni. in g dur. für M:ʳ Morella. Dalla sua pace etc:*
        2 violini, viole, 1 flauto, 2 oboe, 2 Corni, 2 fagotti, e Baßi.

---

[76] K.537 Piano concerto in D, often called the 'Coronation' concerto.

[77] K.538 Aria for soprano and orchestra, 'Ah se in ciel, benigne stelle'.

[78] K.539 Song with orchestral accompaniment, *Ein deutsches Kriegslied.*

[79] K.540 Adagio in B minor for piano.

[80] K.527, No.11 (540a) Aria for tenor, 'Dalla sua pace', for Don Ottavio in the Vienna 1788
        production of *Don Giovanni*

den 28 ! detto

[81] *Ein Duetto zur Oper: Don Giovanni. für Mad.ᵐᵉ Mombelli, und Sig. Benucci,*
     in C Dur. — Per quelle tue Manine etc:
     2 violini, viola, 2 flauti, 2 oboe, 2 fagotti, 2 clarini, e Baßi.

den 30 ! —

[82] *scena zur detta Opera für Mad.ˢᵍ.ˡˡᵉ Cavallieri. — Recit: In quali Ecceßi etc:*
     Aria. — mi tradì quell' alma ingrata. —
     2 violini, viole, 1 flauto, 2 clarinetti, 2 fagotti, 2 Corni, e Baßo.

im Monath May.

[83] *Arietta für M.ʳ Albertarelli in die oper le Gelosie fortunate. un bacio di mano etc:*
     2 violini, 1 flauto, 2 oboe, 2 fagotti, 2 Corni, viole e Baßi.

den 22 ! Juny.

[84] *Ein Terzett für klavier, violin, und Violoncello. —*

den 26: detto.

[85] *Eine Sinfonie. — 2 violini, 1 flauto, 2 clarinetti, 2 fagotti, 2 Corni,*
     2 clarini, timpany, viole e Baßi.

---

[81] K.540b Duet for soprano and bass, 'Per queste tue manine', for Zerlina and Leporello in the
      Vienna 1788 production of *Don Giovanni*.
[82] K.527, No.23 (K.540c) Recitative, 'In quali eccessi', and aria, 'Mi tradì quell'alma ingrata',
      for soprano, Donna Elvira in the Vienna 1788 production of *Don Giovanni*.
[83] K.541 Aria for bass, 'Un bacio di mano', for inclusion in the opera *Le gelosie fortunate* by
      Pasquale Anfossi.
[84] K.542 Trio in E major for piano, violin, and violoncello.
[85] K.543 Symphony in E flat.

—— *detto:*

[86] *Eine kleiner Marsch. 1 volino, 1 flauto, 1 viola, 1 Corno, e Violoncello.*

—— *detto:*

[87] *Eine kleine klavier Sonate für anfänger.*

— *detto.*

[88] *Ein kurzes Adagio. à 2 violini, viola, e Baßo, zu einer fuge welche ich schon lange für 2 klaviere geschrieben habe.*

den 10: Jullius.

[89] *Eine kleine klavier Sonate – für Anfänger mit einer Violin.*

den 14 ̣ detto.

[90] *Ein Terzett für klavier, violin, und violoncello.*

---

[86] K.544 Little march in D, for five instruments. (This work is lost).

[87] K.545 Sonata in C for piano, written for beginners.

[88] K.546 Adagio in C minor for a string orchestra, written and published as a prelude to a C-minor fugue for string orchestra, which was a rearrangement of the two-piano work, K.426.

[89] K.547 Sonata in F for piano and violin, written for beginners.

[90] K.548 Trio in C for piano, violin, and violoncello.

den 16: detto.

[91]   *Eine kleine Canzonette. à 2 soprani e Baßo.*

den 25 ⸽.

[92]   *Eine Sinfonie. —— 2 violini, 1 flautto, 2 oboe, 2 fagotti, 2 Corni, viole*
       e Baßi:

den 10 ⸽ August.

[93]   *Eine Sinfonie. —— 2 violini, 1 flauto, 2 oboe, 2 fagotti, 2 Corni, 2 clarini,*
       Timpany, viole e Baßi. ——

den 11 ᵗᵉⁿ⸽ aug:

[94]   *Ein lied. — beym auszug in das feld. ———*

den 2 ᵗᵉⁿ⸽ Sept:

[95]   *(8). 4stim̄ige Canoni.*

---

[91]   K.549 Canzonetta for two sopranos and bass, perhaps accompanied by three basset-horns,
       'Più non si trovano'.

[92]   K.550 Symphony in G minor.

[93]   K.551 Symphony in C, often called the 'Jupiter' symphony.

[94]   K.552 Song with piano accompaniment, *Beim Auszug in das Feld.*

[95]   K.553, K.554, K.555, K.556, K.557, K.558, K.560, K.561 Eight canons for four voices.

item

[96] *2. 3stimige Canoni.* ——

27 $^!$ item.

[97] *Ein Divertimento à 1 violino, 1 viola, e Violoncello; di sei Pezzi:*

27 $^!$ ocktober.

[98] *Ein Terzett für klavier, violin und Violoncello.* ——

den 30 $^!$ detto.

[99] *2 Contredanses. à 2 violini, 2 oboe, 2 corni, 1 fagotto e Baßo:*

den 6 $^!$ dec:

[100] *6 teutsche.* —— *à 2 violini, 2 flauti, 2 oboe, 2 clarinetti, 2 fagotti,*
       2 corni, 2 clarini, timpany, flauttino e Baßi. ——··

NB: im Monath November Händels Acis und Galathée
   für Baron Suiten bearbeitet.

---

[96] K.559, K.562 Two canons for three voices.

[97] K.563 Divertimento in E flat for violin, viola, and violoncello.

[98] K.564 Trio in G for piano, violin, and violoncello.

[99] K.565 Two contredanses for eight instruments. (These works are lost).

[100] K.567 Six German dances for orchestra.

[NB] K.566 Rescored version of Handel's *Acis and Galatea*.

den 24 ! detto.

[101]   *12 Menuetten. à 2 violini, 2 flauti, 2 oboe, 2 clarinetti, 2 fagotti,*
         2 clarini, Timpany, flauttino, e Baßi.

im Jenner.   1789.

[102]   *Eine teutsche Aria. 2 violini, viole, 2 oboe, 2 fagotti, 2 corni,*
         e Baßi. — Ohne zwang aus eignem Triebe etc:

im februar.

[103]   *Eine Sonate auf klavier allein.*

den 21 ! detto

[104]   *6 teutsche. —— à 2 violini, 2 flauti, 2 oboe, 2 clarinetti, 2 fagotti,*
         2 clarini, timpany, flauttino, e Baßi, und türkische Musick.

29 ! aprill. in Potsdam.

[105]   *6 variazionen auf das klavier allein. über einen Menuett vom Duport.*

NB: im Monath März für Baron Suiten Händels Messias
     bearbeitet.

---

[101]   K.568 Twelve minuets for orchestra.

[102]   K.569 Aria for soprano(?) and orchestra, 'Ohne Zwang, aus eignem Triebe'. (This work
         is lost).

[103]   K.570 Piano sonata in B flat.

[104]   K.571 Six German dances for orchestra.

[105]   K.573 Nine (not merely six) variations for piano on a minuet by Jean Pierre Duport.

[NB]   K.572 Rescored version of Handel's *Messiah*.

17 ! May. in Leipzig.

[106] _Eine kleine Gigue für das klavier. in das Staṁbuch des Hr: Engel._
       kurfürst: Sächsischen HofOrganisten in Leipzig.

im Junius. in Wienn.

[107] _Ein Quartett für 2 violin, viola et violoncello. für Seine Mayestätt dem_
       könig in Preussen.

im Jullius.

[108] _Eine Sonate auf klavier allein._

---

[109] _Ein Rondò in meine Oper figaro für Mad.ᵐᵉ ferarese del bene. —_
       2 violini, viole, 2 corni di Baßetto; 2 fagotti, 2 Corni, e Baßi.

im August.

[110] _Eine Aria in die Oper. I Due Baroni. für Mad.ˢᵉˡˡᵉ Louise Villeneuve._
       2 violini, viole, 2 oboe, 2 fagotti, 2 Corni, e Baßi. — Alma grande, e nobil Core e

---

[106] K.574 Little Gigue in G for piano.

[107] K.575 String quartet in D (the first 'Prussian' quartet).

[108] K.576 Piano sonata in D.

[109] K.577 Rondò for soprano, 'Al desio, di chi t'adora', for Susanna in the 1789 revival of _Figaro_
       in Vienna.

[110] K.578 Aria for soprano, 'Alma grande e nobil core', for inclusion in the opera _I due Baroni_
       by Domenico Cimarosa.

den 17 ! September.

[111] *Eine Aria in die Oper. der balbier von Seviglien. für Mad.ᵐᵉ Hoffer.*
    2 violini, viole, 2 clarinetti, 2 fagotti. 2 corni e Baßi. —
    Schon lacht der holde frühling.

den 29 ! detto.

[112] *Ein Quintett. à 1 clarinetto, 2 violini, viola e violoncello.*

im ocktober.

[113] *Eine Arie in die Oper: Il Burbero. für Madˢᵉˡˡᵉ Villeneuve.*
    2 violini, 2 clarinetti, 2 fagotti, 2 corni, viole e Baßi.
    chi sà chi sà qual sia etc:

detto —— —— —— ——

[114] *Vado! ma dove? – oh Dio! etc:*

im December.

[115] *Eine arie welche in die Oper Così fan tutte bestim̄t war, für*
    Benuccì. Rivolgete à me lo sguardo etc: —
    2 violini, viola, 2 oboe, 2 fagotti, 2 clarini e Timpany e Baßi:

---

[111] K.580 Aria for soprano, 'Schon lacht der holde Frühling', for inclusion in a German
    language production of the opera *Il Barbiere di Siviglia* by Paisiello.

[112] K.581 Quintet in A for clarinet and string quartet.

[113] K.582 Aria for soprano, 'Chi sà, chi sà, qual sia', for inclusion in the opera *Il Burbero di buon
    cuore* by Vicente Martin.

[114] K.583 Aria for soprano, 'Vado, ma dove? – oh Dei!', for inclusion in the opera *Il Burbero
    di buon cuore* by Vicente Martin.

[115] K.584 Aria for bass, 'Rivolgete a lui lo sguardo', for Guglielmo in *Così fan tutte,* but not
    included in the opera.

im Decembre.

[116] *12 Menuetts. à 2 violini, 2 flauti, 2 oboe, 2 clarinetti, 2 fagotti, 2 corni,*
          2 clarini, timpany, flauttino e Baßo:

detto

[117] *12 teutsche. ai nedem̄i Istromenti. NB einen Contredanse. der*
                        Sieg vom Helden koburg.

im Jenner. *1790:*

[118] *Così fan tutte; osia la scuola degli amanti. Opera Buffa in 2 Atti.*
          pezzi di Musica. ____ . Attori. Signore. ferraresi del Bene, Villeneuve et
          Bußani. Signori Calvesti, Benucci e Bußani.

im May

[119] *Ein Quartett. für 2 violin, viola e violoncello.*

im Junnius.

[120] *Ein Quartett. für 2 violin, viola e Violoncello.*

NB: im Monath Jullius Händels Caecilia und Alexanders-
      fest für B: Suiten bearbeitet.

---

[116] K.585 Twelve minuets for orchestra.

[117] K.586 Twelve German dances for orchestra.

[117, **NB**] K.587 Contredanse for a small orchestra, called 'Der Sieg vom Helden Coburg'.

[118] K.588 *Così fan tutte,* comic opera in 2 acts, first performed in Vienna on 26 January 1790.

[119] K.589 String quartet in B flat (the second 'Prussian' quartet).

[120] K.590 String quartet in F (the third 'Prussian' quartet).

[**NB**] K.592, K.591 Rescored versions of Handel's *Ode for St. Cecilia's Day,* and *Alexander's Feast.*

im Decembre.

[121] *Ein Quintett. für 2 violin, 2 viola e Violoncello.*

[122] *Ein Stück für ein Orgelwerk in einer uhr.* ___

5 $\overset{ten}{:}$ *Jenner.*

1791.

[123] *Ein klavier=konzert. begleitung. — 2 violini, 1 flauto, 2 oboe,*

2 fagotti – 2 corni, viole e Baßi.

14 $\overset{ten}{:}$

[124]   *Sehnsucht nach dem frühlinge.   Im frühlings Anfange.*

3 teutsche lieder. —— komm, lieber May. etc: Erwacht zum neuen Leben. etc:

das kinderspiel.

Wir kinder, wir schmecken der freude recht viel. etc.

23 $\overset{ten}{:}$

[125] *6 Menuetti für die Redoute.* ___ *mit allen Stim̄en.*

---

[121] K.593 String quintet in D.

[122] K.594 Adagio and Allegro in F minor for a mechanical organ.

[123] K.595 Piano concerto in B flat.

[124] K.596, K.597, K.598 Three songs for the children's song-book 'Frühlingslieder', *Sehnsucht nach dem Frühling, Im Frühlingsanfang,* and *Das Kinderspiel.*

[125] K.599 Six minuets for orchestra.

den 29 ! ——

[126] *6 teutsche. —— mit allen Stimen.*

den 5 ! —— Hornung.

[127] *4 Menuett, und 4 teutsche.*

item.

[128] *zwey kontertänze. ——*

den 12 ! ——

[129] *2 Menuett, und 2 teutsche. ——*

den 28 ! ——

[130] *1 Contre-Danse. Il Trionfo delle Donne. und 6 Landlerische.*

---

[126]   K.600 Six German dances for orchestra.

[127]   K.601, K.602 Four minuets and four German dances for orchestra.

[128]   K.603 Two contredanses for orchestra.

[129]   K.604 and K.605, nos. 1 & 2 Two minuets and two German dances for orchestra.

[130]   K.607 (K.605a), K.606 Contredanse for a small orchestra, called 'Il Trionfo delle Donne'; and six slow waltzes for two violins and bass.

den 3! März.

[131] *Ein OrgelStücke für eine Uhr. —*

den 6! ——

[132] *1 Contredanse. die leyerer. — 1 teutscher mit leyerer trio.*

den 8ᵗᵉⁿ —

[133] *Eine Baß Aria mit obligatem Contra Baß. —— für H: Görl und Pischlberger.*
Per questa bella Mano etc: etc:

———————

[134] *Variazionen auf das klavier über das Lied: Ein Weib ist das herrlichste ding etc: etc:*

den 12ᵗᵉⁿ Aprill

[135] *Ein Quintett für 2 violin, 2 viole, violoncello.*

———————

[131] K.608 Allegro and Andante in F minor for a mechanical organ.

[132] K.610, K.611 Contredanse for a small orchestra, called 'Les filles malicieuses', and German
dance for orchestra.

[133] K.612 Aria for bass, with orchestral accompaniment, 'Per questa bella mano'.

[134] K.613 Eight variations for piano on the song 'Ein Weib ist das herrlichste Ding auf der
Welt', in a play by Schikaneder.

[135] K.614 String quintet in E flat.

den 20 ! Aprill.

[136] *Einen SchlußChor in die Oper. Le Gelosie Vilane vom Sarti.*
       für dilettanti. —— Viviamo felici in dolce Contento. etc etc.

den 4 ! May.

[137] *Ein Andante für eine Walze in eine kleine Orgel.*

den 23 ! May.

[138] *Adagio und Rondeau für Harmonica, 1 flauto, 1 oboe,*
       1 viola, e Violoncello

den 18 ! Juñius. in Baaden.

[139] *Ave verum Corpus., —— à canto, Alto, tenore, Baßo. —— 2 violini, viola,*
       organo e Baßi. _____

im Jullius

[140] *Eine kleine teutsche kantate für eine Stime am klavier.*
       die ihr des unermesslichen Weltals schöpfer Ehrt etc etc.

---

[136] K.615 Final chorus, 'Viviamo felici in dolce contento', for Giuseppe Sarti's opera *Le gelosie villane*. (This work is lost).

[137] K.616 Andante in F for a mechanical organ.

[138] K.617 Adagio and Rondo for glass harmonica, flute, oboe, viola, and violoncello.

[139] K.618 Motet, *Ave verum corpus*, for 4 voices, 4 strings, and organ.

[140] K.619 Little German cantata, 'Die ihr des unermesslichen Weltalls Schöpfer ehrt', with piano accompaniment.

Im Jullius.

141] *die Zauberflöte. —— aufgeführt den 30ᵗ September.*

— — — — — — — — eine teutsche Oper in 2 Aufzügen. von Eman. Schickaneder.
bestehend in 22 Stücken. — frauenzimer. —— Mad^{selle}: Gottlieb. Mad^{me}: Hofer. Mad^{me}: Görl.
Mad^{ll}: klöpfler. Mad^{selle}: HofMann. Männer. Hr: Schack. Hr: Görl. Hr: Schickaneder der ältere.
Hr: kistler. Hr: Schickaneder der Jüngere. Hr: Nouseul. — Chöre.

den 5ᵗ September. — aufgeführt in Prag den 6ᵗ September.

142] *La Clemenza di Tito. opera Seria in Due Atti. per l'incoron=*
nazione di sua Maestá l'imperatore Leopoldo II. —— ridotta á
vera opera dal Sig^{re}: Mazzolá. Poeta di sua A: S: l'Elettore di
Saßonia. —— Atrici:— Sig^{ra}: Marchetti fantozi. —— Sig^{ra}: Antonini.
—— Attori. Sig^{re}: Bedini. Sig^{ra}: Carolina Perini / da Uomo / Sig^{re}:
Baglioni. Sig^{re}: Campi. — e Cori. —— 24 Pezzi. ——

den 28ᵗ September.

143] *zur Oper. die Zauberflöte —— einen PriesterMarsch und die Ouverture.*

144] *Ein konzert für die Clarinette. für Hr: Stadler den Ältern.*
begleitung. 2 violin, viole, 2 flauti, 2 fagotti, 2 Corni e Baßi.

den 15ᵗ Novembr.

145] *Eine kleine freymaurer=kantate. bestehend aus 1 Chor. 1 Arie.*
2 Recitativen, und ein Duo. tenor und Baß,
2 violin, viole, Baßo, 1 flauto, 2 oboe e 2 Corni. ——

141] K.620 *Die Zauberflöte* ('The Magic Flute'), German opera in 2 acts, first performed in Vienna on 30 September 1791.

142] K.621 *La Clemenza di Tito*, opera seria in 2 acts, first performed in Prague on 6 September 1791.

143] K.620 The priests' march, and the overture, for *Die Zauberflöte*.

144] K.622 Clarinet concerto in A.

145] K.623 Masonic cantata, 'Laut verkünde unsre Freude', for 2 tenors, bass, and small orchestra.

THE FACSIMILE

1784.

Den 9ten Hornung.

1, + Ein Klavierkonzert - begleitung - 2 violini, viola e Basso. (2 oboe, 2 corni ad lib...

Den 15ten März.

2, Ein Klavier Konzert. begleitung. 2 violini e 2 viole, i flauto, 2 oboe, 2 fagotti, 2 Corni e Basso.

Den 22ten.

+3, + Ein Klavierkonzert. begleitung. 2 violini, 2 viole, i flauto. 2 oboe, 2 fagotti, 2 corni, 2 Clarini, Timpani e Basso.

Den 30ten.

4, Ein Klavier Quintett. begleitung. i oboe, i clarinetto, i corno, et i fagotto.

Den 12ten April.

+5+ Ein Klavier Konzert. begleitung. 2 violini, 2 viole, i flauto, 2 oboe, 2 fagotti, 2 corni, e Basso.

Allegro
oboe e fagotti
pia:
All.
violini
All.
pia:
Largo
pia:
f
All.
pia:
pia

Den 2⟨5⟩ Juli.

+ 6, + Eine Clavier Sonate mit einer Violin.
+

Den 25. August.

+ 7 + 10 Variazionen für das Clavier allein.
+

Den 30. September.

+ 8 + Ein Clavier Conzert. Begleitung: 2 Violini, 2 Viole, 1 flauto, 2 oboe, 2 fagotti,
+   2 Corni e Basso.

Den 14t. Oktober.

+ 9 + Eine Sonate für das Clavier allein.
+

Den 9ten November.

+ 10 + Ein Quartett für 2 Violini, viola e violoncello.
+

Den 11ten December.

+ Ein Clavier Conzert. begleitung. 2 Violini, 2 Viole, 1 flauto, 2 oboe, 2 fagotti,
+ 2 Corni, 2 Clarini, timpany e Basso.

1785.

Den 10ten Jenner.

+ + Ein Quartett für 2 violini, viola e violoncello.
+

Den 14ten:

+ + Ein Quartett für 2 violini, viola e Violoncello.
+

Den 10ten Hornung.

Ein Clavier Conzert. begleitung. 2 Violini, 2 Viole, 1 flauto, 2 oboe,
2 fagotti, 2 Corni, 2 Clarini, timpany e Basso.

Den 6ten März.

+ + Eine Arie für Ledembaygar zur Societäts Musique. A te frà tanti affanni etc
+ begleitung. 2 violini, 2 viole, 1 flauto, 1 oboe, 1 clarinetto, 1 fagotti, 2 Corni e Basso.

den 9ten März.

+ Ein Clavier Konzert. Begleitung . 2 violini, 2 viole, 1 flauto, 2 oboe, 2 fagotti,
+ 2 Corni, 2 Clarini, timpany e Basso.

den 11ten

+ Ein Terzett für die Cavaglieri zur Societäts Musique. — Tra l'oscure ombre funest
+ Begleitung. 2 violini, 2 viole, 1 flauto, 2 oboe, 2 fagotti, 2 Corni e Basso.

den 26ten

+ Maurer Gesellen = Lied für Singstimme und Clavier. die ist einem treuen Bruder
+ der Lobrednung nur ein mehr C:

den 1ten Aprill.

Ein Rondeaux für die Violin zu einem Konzert. Begleitung. 2 Violini, Viola,
2 oboe, 2 Corni e Basso.

den 20ten

Eine kleine Kantate. die Maurerfreude. — Singstimme. Tenor. und zum
Schluß ein kleiner Chor von 2 Tenor und einem Bass. Begleitung. 2 violini,
2 viole, 1 clarinetto, 2 oboe, 2 Corni e Basso.

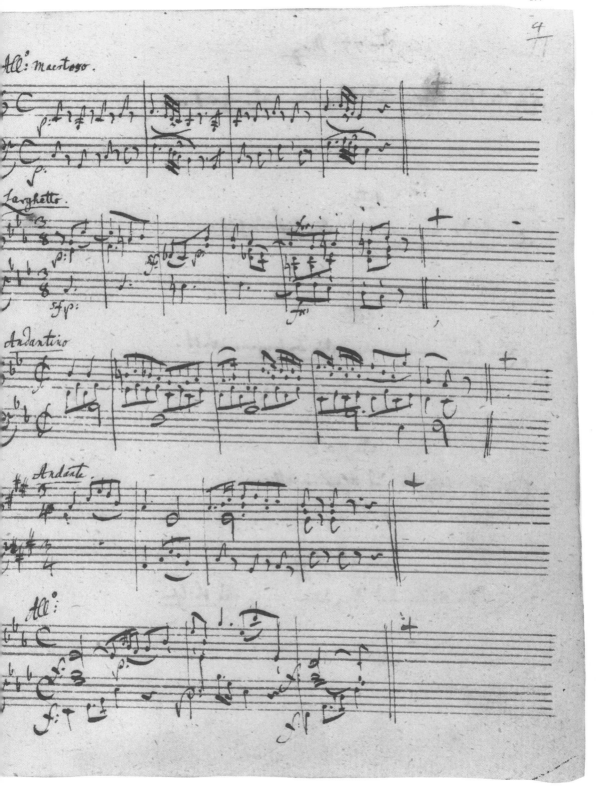

Den 7ten März.

+ Ein Lied für Clavier und Singstimme. Die Zaubrer.

detto.

+ Ein Lied. —————— Die Zufriedenheit.

detto.

+ Ein Lied. —————— Die betrogene Welt.

Den 20ten:

+ Eine Phantasie für das Clavier allein.

den 8ten Juny.

+ Ein Lied für Clavier und Singstimme. —— Das Veilchen.

Ihr Mädchen flieht vermöten Ihr!

Adagio.

im Monath Jully.

+ + Maurerische Trauer-Musik bey dem Todfalle der Brüder Mecklenburg und
+ Esterhazy. — 2 violini, 2 viole, 1 clarinett, 1 Bassethorn, 2 oboe,
2 corni e Basso.

detto.

+ + Ein Quartett für Clavier, 1 Violin, 1 Viola und Violoncello.

den 5:ten November.

+ +Quartetto in die Opera. La villanella rapita. für sigra Coltellini, sigr
+ Calvesi, sigr Mandini e Bussani. Begleitung: 2 violini, 2 viole, 2 obo
2 clarinetti, 2 fagotti, 2 corni e Basso.

den 21:ten

+ +Terzetto in detta Opera. für sigra Coltellini, sigr Calvesi e Mandini.
+ Begleitung. 2 violini, 2 viole, 2 flauti, 2 oboe, 2 clarinetti, 2 fagotti,
2 corni e Basso.

den 12:ten December.

Ein Clavier Concert mit Begleitung einer Violin.

den 16.ten december.

Ein Clavier Konzert. Begleitung. 2 Violini, 2 Viole, i flauto, 2 clarinetti,
2 fagotti, 2 Corni, 2 clarini, Timpany e Basso.

1786.
den 3.ten Hornung.

Der Schauspiel Direktor. ein Comödie mit Musick für Schönbrun. bestehend aus ouver:
2 Lieder, ein Terzett und Vaudeville. — für Mad:^{me} Lange, Mad:^{selle} Cavaglieri
und Mr Adamberger.

den 2.ten Mörz.

Ein Clavier Konzert. Begleitung. 2 Violini, 2 Viole, i flauto, 2 Clarine
2 fagotti, 2 Corni e Basso.

den 10.ten

Ein Duetto zu meiner Oper Idomeneo. für die sr: von Pufendorf und Bar: Pulini
Begleitung. 2 Violini, 2 Viole, 2 oboe, 2 fagotti, 2 Corni e Basso.

datto.

Scena con Rondò mit violin solo für Bar: Pulini und Graf Hatzfeld in
die obenbemeldte Oper. Begleitung. 2 Violini, 2 viole, 2 clarinetti,
2 fagotti, 2 Corni e Basso.

All°
Corni
Fagotti
Ouverture
All°: assai.
All°
3za:
Andante
Elia
Spiegarti oh Dio non posso
All°: assai.

Den 24ten Märˑz.

+ Ein Clavier Conzert - Begleitung . 2 violini, 2 viola, i flauto, 2 oboè, 2 clarinetti, 2 fagotti, 2 corni, 2 clarini, timpany e Basso.

Den 29t April .

Le Nozze di figaro . opera buffa in 4 Atti. + Pezzi di Musica . 34 . Attori. Signore . Storace, + Laschi, mandini, Bussani e Nanina gottlieb. — sig.ri Benucci, mandini, occhely, e Bussani . —

den 3t Juny .

Ein Quatett für Clavier, violin, viola und Violoncello .

den 10t Juny.

Ein kleines Rondò für das Clavier allein .

den 26ten.

Ein Waldhorn Conzert für den Leitgeb. Begleitung . 2 Violini, 2 viola, 2 oboè, 2 Corni e Basso.

Den 8ten Jully.

+ Ein Terzett für Clavier, violin und Violoncello.

Den 1ten August.

+ Eine Clavier Sonata auf 4 Hände.

Den 5ten

+ Ein Terzett für Clavier, clarinett und Viola.

Den 19ten

+ Ein Quartett für 2 Violin, viola und Violoncello.

Den 12ten September

12 Variazionen für das Clavier allein.

den 4ten November.

+ Variazionen für das Clavier. auf 4 Händt.

den 18ten

+ Ein Terzett für Clavier, violin und Violoncello.

den 4ten december

+ Ein Clavier Konzert. Begleitung. 2 Violini, 2 Viole, i flauto, 2 oboe,
2 fagotti, 2 Corni, 2 Clarini, timpany e Basso.

den 6ten

Eine Sinfonia. — 2 Violini, 2 Viole, 2 flauti, 2 oboe, 2 Corni, 2 fagotti
2 Clarini, timpany e Basso.

den 27ten

Scena con Rondò mit Clavier solo. für Mad:elle storace und mich. Begleitung. 2 Violini,
2 Viole, 2 clarinetti, 2 fagotti, 2 Corni e Basso.

10
Andante
All:°
All:° maestoso
Adagio
Andantino
Recitativo
Rondò
Violino

1787.

in Prag
den 6ten Februar.

+ + 6 Tänzße. 2 Violini, 2 flauti, 1 flauto piccolo, 2 oboe, 2 clarinetti, 2 fagotti
+ 2 Corni, 2 clarini, timpany e Basso.

Wien.
den 11te März.

+ + Ein Rondò für das Clavier allein.

den 18ten

Scena für fl: Fischer. non so d'onde viene C: Tekstiting. 2 Violini, 2 Viole,
1 flauto, 2 oboe, 2 fagotti, 2 Corni e Basso.

den 23ten

+ Eine Aria für fl: gottfried von Jacquin. Mentre ti lascio o figlia C:
Tekstiting. 2 Violini, 2 Viole, 1 flauto, 2 clarinetti, 2 fagotti, 2 Corni e Basso

den 19ten Decemb.

+ + Ein Quintett für 2 Violini, 2 Viole und Violoncello.

den 16ten März.

Ein Quintett für 2 Violin, 2 Viola und Violoncello.

den 18ten

Ein Lied für Klavier und Singstimme. die Delta.

den 20ten

Ein Lied ———— die Verzweigung. ————

den 23ten

Ein Lied. ——— die Sammlung.

den 26ten

Ein Lied. ———— alt Lieb die Briefe spat ungetreuer Liebherrad hiebeannte.

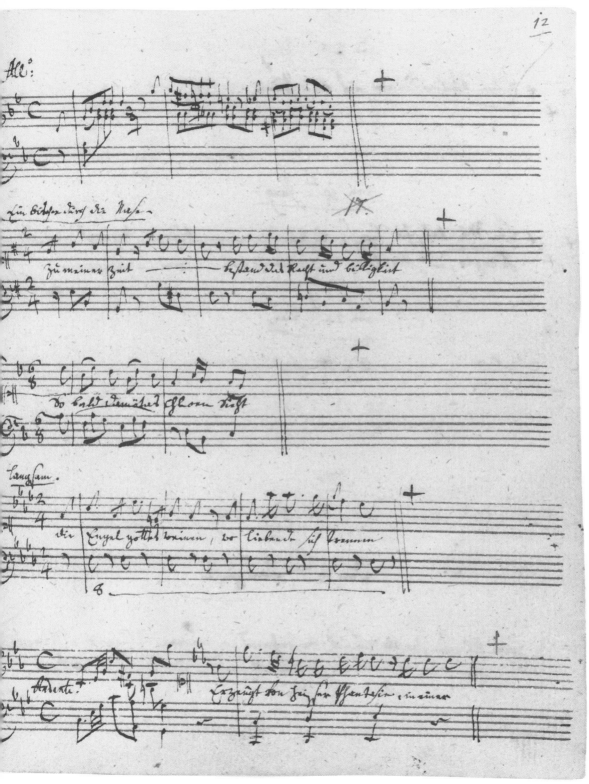

den 29ten März.

+ + Eine kleine Sonate auf die Heyde.

den 14ten Juny.

+ + Ein Musikalischer Spaß; bestehend in einem Allegro, Menuet und Trio,
+ Adagio, und Finale. — 2 violini, viola, 2 corni, e Basso.

den 24ten Juny.

— Ein Lied. — — Abendempfindung.

Ditto.

— Ein Lied. — — An Chloe. —

den 10ten August

Eine kleine Nacht Musick, bestehend in einem Allegro, Menuet
und Trio. — Romance. Menuett und Trio, und Finale.
— 2 violini, viola e Bassi.

18.

19.

den 24ten

+ Eine Klavier Sonate mit begleitung einer Violin.

den 28ten October.

in Prag.

Il dissoluto punito, o, il Don Giovanni. opera Buffa in 2 Atti.

Pezzi di musica. 24. Attori. Signore. Teresa Saporiti, Bondini, e Micelli

Signori. Bassi, Ponziani, Baglioni e Lolli. —

den 3ten November.

Scena für Madme Duschek. Recitativo; — Bella mia fiamma. — Aria. Res

O Cara Ce begleitung

den 6ten

+ Ein lied. — — — Dem Geburtstag des frühl.

+ Ein lied. — — detto das Traumlied.

den 11:t Decbre

✝ Ein Lied. — die kleine Spinnerin. —

den 3t Jenner 1788 -

Ein Allegro und Andante für das Clavier allein.

den 14t detto.

Einen Contretanse. der Donnerwetter. à 2 violini, 2 oboe, 2 Corni, 1 flautino, 1 tromba, und Basso.

den 23t —

Einen Contretanse. die Bataille. — à 2 violini, 2 oboe, 1 flautino, 1 tromba, 1 tromba e Basso.

den 27t —

6 Teütsche. — à 2 violini, 2 flauti, 2 oboe, 2 clarinetti, 2 fagotti, 2 clarini, timpani, flautino e Bassi. —

Den 24.ten Feb:

+ + Ein Klavier Konzert in D dur. — à 2 violini, viola e Basso.
+ 1 flauto, 2 oboe, 2 fagotti, 2 Corni, 2 clarini et timpany ad libitum

Den 4.ten März:

+ + Eine Scena in f dur. — Ah se in ciel benigne stelle C: für Madme Lange
+ begleitung. 2 violini, 2 oboe, 2 fagotti, 2 Corni, viola e Basso.

Den 5.ten

Ein deutsches Kriegs-lied für den jungen Baumann, Schauspieler in der Leopold= d
in A. — Ihr unsre hohe der Kaiser seyn C: begleitung. 2 violini, 2 oboe, 2 Corni,
2 fagotti, 1 flauto piccolo. Piatti, Tamburo grande, viole e Bassi. —

Den 19.ten —

+ Ein Adagio für das Klavier allein. in H mol. —
+

Den 24.ten April.

Eine Scena gia Opera: Don Giovanni — für Madme Morella. Della sua pace C
2 violini, viole, 1 flauto, 2 oboe, 2 Corni, 2 fagotti, e Bassi.

22.

Dalla sua pace la mia di=pen=de

76

den 28! detto

Ein Duetto für opera: Don Giovanni. für Madme Mombelli, und Sig. Benu
in Due. — per quelle tue manine C
2 violini. viola, 2 flauti, 2 oboe, 2 fagotti, 2 clarini, e Bassi.

den 30!

Scena für detta Opera für Madsella Cavallieri. — Recit: la quale Ecce
Aria. — mi tradi quell'alma ingrata. —
2 violini, viole, 1 flauto, 2 clarinetti, 2 fagotti, 2 Corni, e Basso.

im Monath März.

Arietta für Mr: Albertarelli in d. opra le gelosie fortunate. Un bacio di mano
2 violini, 1 flauto, 2 oboe, 2 fagotti, 2 Corni, viole e Bassi.

den 22! Juny.

Ein Terzett für Klavier, violin, und Violoncello. —

den 26: detto
Eine Sinfonia. — 2 violini, 1 flauto, 2 clarinetti, 2 fagotti, 2 Corni,
2 Clarini, Limpany, viole e Bassi.

84

23.
All° moderato
Per quelle tue manine
Rec:
All°
Rondò
mi tra = di quell' alma ingrata qual
Allegretto
un bacio di mano
All°
24.
Adagio

— detto:

Ein kleiner Marsch · i violino, i flauto, i viola i Corno, e Violoncello.

— detto:

Eine kleine Clavier Sonata für anfänger.

— detto.

Ein Einzel Adagio. à 2 Violini, viola e Basso, zu einer fuge welche ich
schon lange für 2 Clavier geschrieben habe.

Den 10: Jullius.

Eine kleine Clavier Sonata für anfänger mit einer Violin.

Den 14t detto.

Ein Terzett für Clavier, Violin und Violoncello.

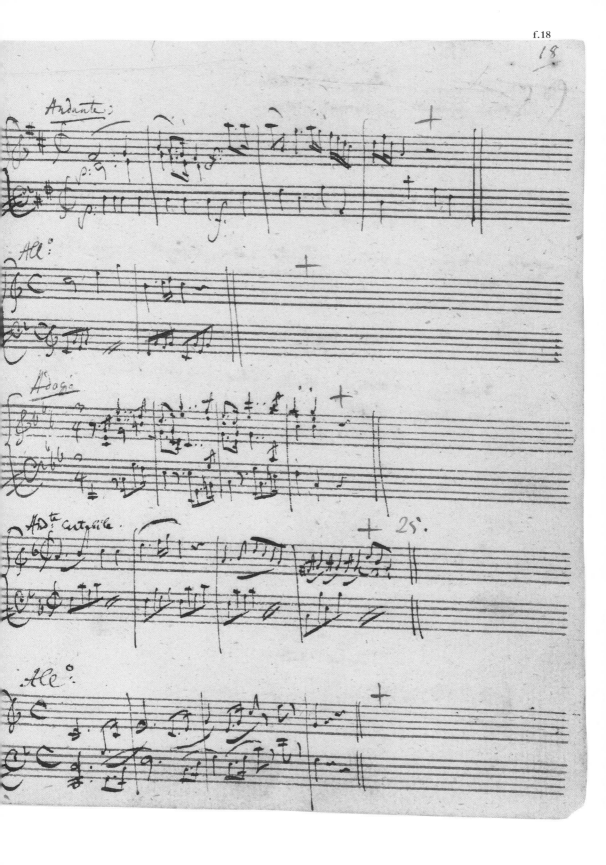

den 16. detto.

L'ultima Canzonetta. à 2 soprani e Basso.

Den 25:.

+ + Eine Sinfonia. — 2 violini, 1 flautto, 2 oboe, 2 fagotti, 2 Corni, viole
  + e Bassi:

Den 10: August.

+ + Eine Sinfonia. — 2 violini, 1 flauto, 2 oboe, 2 fagotti, 2 Corni, 2 clarini,
    Tympany, viole e Bassi. ——

den 11t aug:

Ein Lied. —— Enzian vierzig in dal fald : ———

den 2t Sept:

(8.) 4 stimmige Canoni.

item

2. 3 stimige Caroni.

27¹: item.

Ein Divertimento à i violino, i viola, e Violoncello; di sei Perri:

27¹: october.

+ Ein Terzett fürs Clavier, violin und Violoncello. —

Den 30¹: detto.

2 Contradansen. à 2 violini, 2 oboe, 2 corni, i fagotto e Basso:

den 6¹: dec:

6 Märsche. — à 2 violini, 2 flauti, 2 oboe, 2 clarinetti, 2 fagotti, 2 corni, 2 clarini trompeny, flauttino e Bassi. —

NB: im Monath november zum Acis und Galathée für Baron Seiten überbricht.

Den 24t: detto.

100 12 Menuetten. à 2 violini, 2 flauti, 2 oboe, 2 clarinetti, 2 fagotti, 2 clarini, Timpany, flauttino, e Bassi.

im Januar — 1789.

101 Eine deutsche Aria. 2 violini Viole, 2 oboe, 2 fagotti, 2 corni, e Bassi: — Ohne gesang mit eignem Biech C:

im Februar.

102 Eine Sonata auf Clavier allein.

Den 21t: detto

6 deutsche. — à 2 violini, 2 flauti, 2 oboe, 2 clarinetti, 2 fagotti, 2 clarini; Timpany, flauttino, e Bassi, und türkische Musik.

29t april. in Potsdam.

6 variationen auf das Clavier allein. über einen Menuett von Duport

NB: im Monath März für Baron lieben Zaudall Meßius überschrieben.

17t May. in Leipzig.

Eine kleine Gigue für das Clavier. in das Stammbuch des Hn: Engel
Churfürst: Sächsischen Hof Organisten in Leipzig.

im Jenner. in May.

Ein Quartett für 2 violin, viola et Violoncello. für Seine Majestätt dem
König in Preußen.

im Jullius.

Eine Sonate auf Clavier allein.

Ein Rondò in meine Opera figaro für Madme Ferarese del bene. —
2 violini, viola, 2 corni di Bassetto i 2 fagotti, 2 Corni, e Bassi.

im August.

Eine Aria in die Opera. I Due Baroni für Madelle Louise Villeneuve
2 violini, viola, 2 oboe, 2 fagotti, 2 Corni, e Bassi. — Alma grande, e nobil core

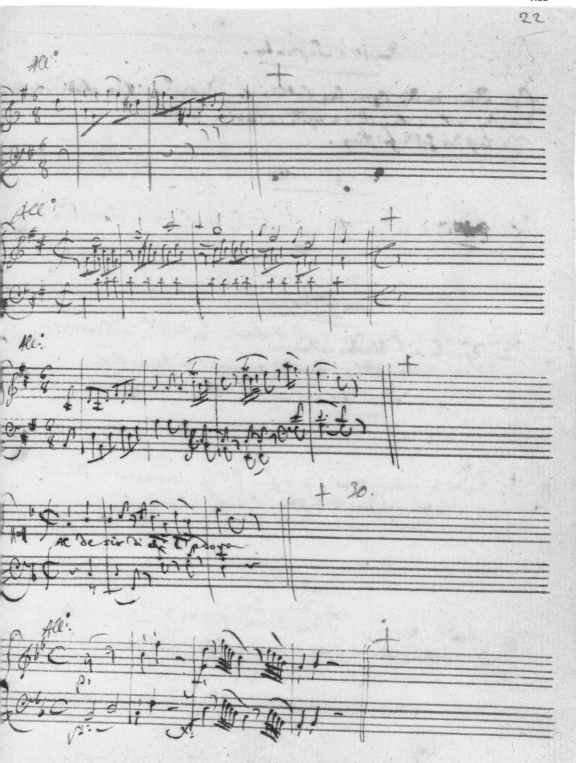

Den 17: September.

Eine Arie in die Opra: des Cecilio don Dotigliani. für Made: Hofer
2 violini, viola, 2 clarinetti, 2 fagotti, 2 Corni e Baßi. —
Schon lacht der holde frühling.

Den 29: detto.

Ein Quintett à 1 clarinetto, 2 violini, viola e violoncello.

im octtober.

Eine Arie in die Opra: Il Burbero. für Madselle: Villeneuve.
2 violini, 2 clarinetti, 2 fagotti, 2 corni, viola e Baßi.
Chi sà chi sà qual sia

Detto —
Vado! ma dove? — oh Dio!

im December.

Eine arie welche in die Opra così fan tutte bestimt war. für
Benucci. Rivolgete à me lo squardo. —
2 violini, viola, 2 oboe, 2 fagotti, 2 clarini e Timpany e Baßi:

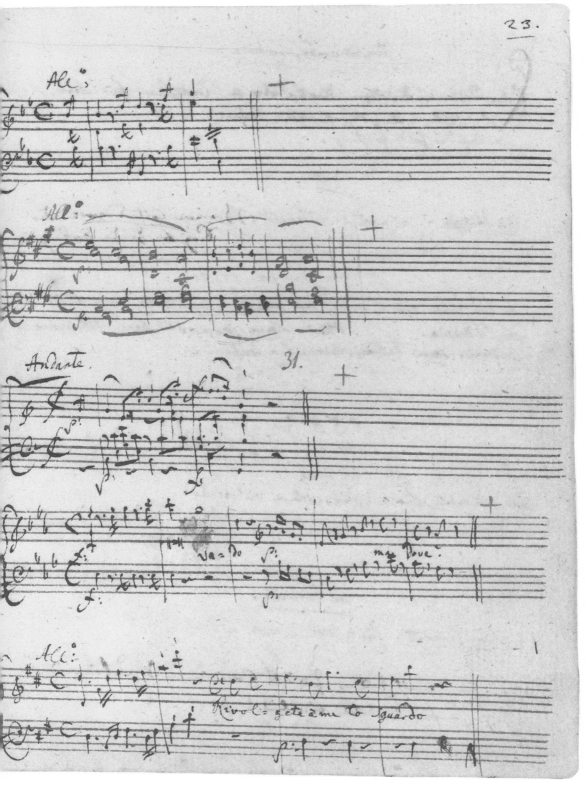

Va do

mia Dove.

Rivol: gete à mi: lo guardo

im December.

12 Menuetti. à 2 violini, 2 flauti, 2 oboe, 2 clarinetti, 2 fagotti, 2 corni,
2 clarini, Timpany, flauttino e Basso:

detto.

12 Teütsche. ai medemi Istromenti. Worin Contradansce etc
Piva ben halten cobüey.

im Jenner. 1790:

Così fan tutte; ossia la scuola degli amanti. Opera Buffa in 2 Atti.
pezzi di Musica. ── Attori. Signore. Ferraresi del Bene, Villeneuve et
Bussani. Signori Calvesi, Benucci e Bussani.

im März.

† Ein Quartett. für 2 Violin, viola e violoncello.

im Jenner.

† Ein Quartett. für 2 violin, viola e Violoncello.

N: im Monath Jullius händel Cäcilia und Alexanderfest
für B: Sister tamlichet.

119

32.

Allegretto

Ouverture. Andante Maestoso:

All°:

Alli Moderato:

im Decembre.

+ Ein Quintett. für 2 violin, viola e violoncello.

Ein Stück für ein Orgelwerk in einer Uhr. ——

5 ^{ten} Jenner.
1791.

+ Ein Clavier= Conzert. begleitung. — 2 violini, 1 flauto, 2 oboe,
+ 2 fagotti — 2 corni, viola e Bassi.

14 ^{ten}

Sehnsucht nach dem Frühlinge.   Im Frühlingsanfange.
3 teutsche Lieder. — Komm, lieber May :C: Erwacht zum neuen Leben. :C:
                    das Kinderspiel.
Wir Kinder, wir schmecken der Freuden recht viel. :C:

23 ^{ten}

6 Menuetti für die Redoute. — mit allen Stimen.

Den 29t —

6 Teütsche. — mit allen Trinen.

Den 5t Hornung.

4 Menuett, und 4 Teütsche.

_____

item.

Zwanzig Contratänze. —

Den 12t —

2 Menuett und 2 Teütsche. —

Den 28t —

+) Contra-Tanz. Il Trionfo delle Donne. und 6 Ländlerische.

†
†

129

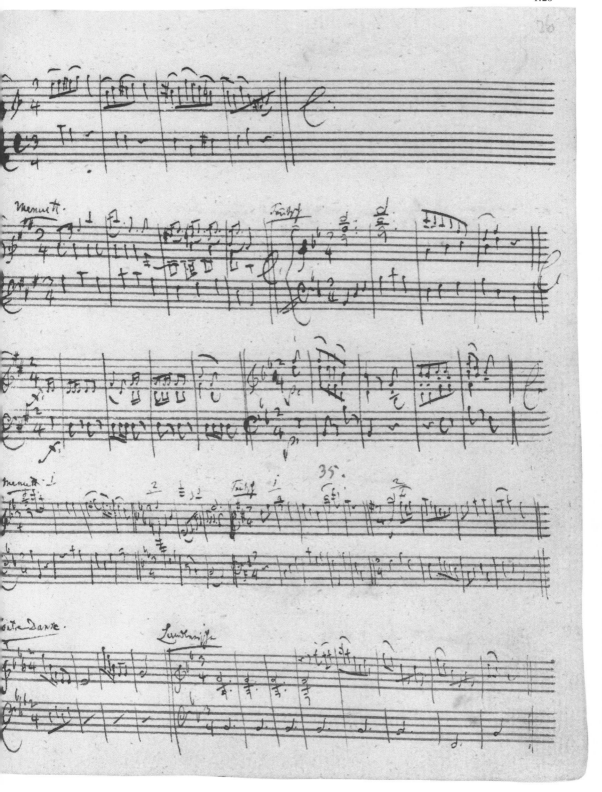

von d.. März.

Ein Orgelstück für eine Uhr. ———

Den 6.. ——

1 Contradanc. ... —— ... mit ... Trio.

Den 8.. ——

Eine Baß Aria mit obligaten Contra-Baß. —— für ... und ...
Per questa bella mano C. C.

Variationen auf dem Clavier über das Lied: ...

Den 12.. ...

Ein Quintett für 2 Violin, 2 Viole, Violoncello.

Am 20t. April.

Einen Schlußchor in der Oper. Le Gelosie Vilane von Sart.
für Dilettanti. — Viviamo felici in dolce Contento. C. C.

den 4t. März.

Ein Andante für einen Walze in einer kleinen Orgel.

Den 23t. März.

Adagio und Rondeau für Harmonica, 1 flauto, 1 oboe,
1 Viola, e Violoncello.

den 18t. Junius. in Dresden.

+ Ave verum Corpus, — à Canto, Alto, Tenore Baßo. — 2 Violini, Viola
Organo e Baßi. ——

im Jullius.

Eine kleine deutsche Kantate für eine Stime, un Clavier.
Die ihr des unermeßlichen Weltalls Schöpfer ehrt C. C.

Im Jullius.

Die Zauberflöte. — aufgeführt den 30:t September.
bestehend in 22 Stücken. — Frauenzimer. — Madselle Gottlieb. Madme Hofer. Madme Gö
Madselle Klöpfler. Madselle Hofmann. Mäner. Hr. Schack. Hr. Göhl. Hr. Schikaneder der älte.
Hr. Küstler. Hr. Schikaneder der jüngere. Hr. Nouseul. — Chör.

Den 5:t September. — aufgeführt in Prag den 6:t September
La Clemenza di Tito. opera seria in due Atti, per l'incoro
nazione di sua maestá l'imperatore Leopoldo II. — ridotta a
vera opera dal sigr. Mazzolá. Poeta di sua A: S: l'Elettore di
Sassonia. — Attrici: — Sigra. Marchetti fantozi. — Mselle Antonini
— Attori. Sigr. Bedini. Sigra. Carolina Perini /dall'omo/ Sigr.
Baglioni. Sigr. Campi. — e Cori. — 24 Pezzi. —

Den 28:t September.
zur Oper die Zauberflöte — einen Priestermarsch und die ouverture

Ein Konzert für die Clarinette. für Hr. Stadler den ältern
begleitung. 2 violini, viola, 2 flauti, 2 fagotti, 2 Corni e Bassi.

den 15:t November.

Eine Kleine freymaurer=kantate. bestehend aus 1 Chor. 1 Arie
2 Recitativen, und ein Duo. Tenor und Bass.
2 violini, viola, Bassi, 1 flauto, 2 oboe e 2 Corni. —